Diary of a Victo1

The Journal of Octavia Grimston (1845 - 1926)

With an introduction by Arthur C. Ventress

Contents

Part One: The Pyrenees and the return to Kilnwick via Paris and London

Part Two: A Small Episode in My Life Written from Recollection

Part Three: My Visit to Ireland, May, 1866

Part Four: A Glimpse into Scotland and the Lake District, Autumn, 1866

Part Five: My Wedding, Beginning from the Sunday Before, Jan 6th, 1867

Part Six: My Honeymoon in France & Italy

Part Seven: Married Life

Introduction

On 1st February 2007, at an antiques fair near Lincoln, I bought a tatty, dull-looking brown notebook with a broken brass lock dangling from the edge of its cover. This unpromising piece of wreckage, upon closer inspection, turned out to be a Victorian journal written by Octavia Elfrida Grimston, a young woman born into a privileged upper-class family which once resided at Kilnwick Hall and Grimston Garth in the East Riding of Yorkshire. The plan was to transcribe it and uncover the secrets entombed within - secrets which had lain undisturbed for nearly a century and a half. But for several years the road to hell remained unpaved by this good intention, and the journal sat on a shelf, gathering ever more dust. Then, out of left field, came the coronavirus, which has led, as we all know, to the civilised world being overwhelmed by a plague of lockdown-enabled literary projects. I offer no excuse, other than to say that this is not a novel, but a fascinating piece of social history, and contains no creative input from me, other than this introduction and a few notes and observations.

The action begins on Sunday 26th January 1862, when Octavia was a mere 16 years old. The opening scene is the little city of Pau, south-western France, situated close to the Pyrenees and the Spanish border, which in the 19th century, due to its benign though somewhat soggy climate, was a popular overwintering spot for wealthy Brits. The players are other family members, along with numerous friends and acquaintances of the same exclusive class.

The journal contains some short passages written in a simple substitution code, which I have deciphered, and others in a deliberately altered and obscured script which I have found impossible to translate. In fact, Octavia herself expressed a fear that with the passage of time she might forget how this more elaborate system should be interpreted. So those secrets, such as they are, have unfortunately died with her, unless some astute reader can decipher the passages from the photos I have included.

As the daughter of a landed family, Octavia was not required - indeed presumably not permitted - to have any sort of occupation which might have resembled work, and so her young life was one long sightseeing holiday as she travelled round Europe and the UK. It was a dream-like existence of fun and frolics, only brought to an end by a judicious marriage (literally so, as her husband was a barrister) which she entered into with no obvious enthusiasm. Octavia's husband more than made up for her ambivalence, and over the years the couple produced nine children.

Octavia sang, painted, played the piano and wielded the sewing-needle, as all young women of her class were required to do in order to maximise their saleability on the marriage market; but unlike Beatrix Potter, a future neighbour in Bolton Gardens, SW5, where Octavia set up her marital home, she lived and died in affluent obscurity. What follows is a fascinating journey into the mind of a teenage girl nearly a hundred years before 'teenagers' were invented.

Part One
Winter in the Pyrenees

Pau, France, Sunday, January 26, 1862

We were tremendously squashed in church, our girl having come back. Between the services, Kate Costobadie came to walk with Bess, and not only her but her brother, a long boy whose only word while he was here consisted in "Goodbye". Kate wanted either Cis or me to come out too, I suppose to go at the brother, but we were too lazy, so stayed at home. Mama and Jin went to the French service to hear Monsieur Froissart. We were very snug over the fire after church, and slept all the evening.

Pau, Monday, January 27 1862

I read and practiced [*piano*] and painted all the morning, and in the afternoon Jin and I went an exploring walk by Bizanos till we got to the river, where after walking for a piece the loveliness of the place obliged us to sketch. We tried to go on further, but a manufactory withstood us, so we turned homeward instead and sketched the little church from the field. While we were yet engaged in this pursuit, a man came up to us, and after looking over our shoulders began some incoherent questions, which put me in a great fright that the man might be tipsy, but happily Jin soon got up to go away and we came home. The Ottley's party took place in the evening. It was a great squeeze and fearfully oven-like. There were very few nice people there, and Bess and Cis were seized upon when they arrived as great treasures. Everybody seemed bored, and the others were not sorry to come away.

Pau, Tuesday, January 28, 1862

A tribe of Alexanders came yesterday morning, and Constance settled to walk with me today to get moss [*as table decoration*] for their party. So at half-past-two she appeared with Emily and Henry and we set off for the Bizanos wood, filled our baskets and bags and came home again, the children being very tiresome. They came to meet in my room for some time. I showed her my books and my sentences, etc, and at last they departed. I kissed Constance going away. In the evening, Bess and Cis and Mama went to the Alcocks, which they enjoyed more than any before. They danced immensely and had great fun, stayed for the Cotillon and came home at half-past-one. They suspected two cases to be going on, namely Mr Congreve and Rose Spencer, and Mr Lagotellerie and Miss Buchanan, which were great fun to watch.

Pau, Wednesday, January 29, 1862

Went to church and came in late, so sat at the bottom. After church I practiced, and in the afternoon Cis and I went and sketched in the Beaumont's grounds [*Parc Beaumont*] where after a time appeared Mama and Miss MacGregor whom she deposited with us and went on herself. We sat and talked and at last took Miss MacGregor home. In the evening, Jin and Maude went to the Spencers where were some nice people, which made it pleasant.

Maudey had to play, but they came home well pleased.

Pau, Thursday, January 30, 1862

Read and worked in the morning. The afternoon found Jin and me turning into a little path near the castle which led us into the street below. We then turned into the fields near the canal and walked by the river. I scrambled about in odd places under the smaller bridge and was greatly stared at by a glazier boy who passed over my head, but Jin drove him away by coming there herself. We went to the end of the poplars and turned to the right, making our way back through bushes by the river, and had to leap a little stream into which we both got our feet. In the evening, Mama, Bess and Cis went to the Alexanders, which they liked very much, though they hadn't much fun. Cis had a headache all day, which happily went away in time to let her go to the ball. Jin, Maude and I spent the evening in sweet slumber, which was very pleasant indeed!

Pau, Friday, January 31, 1862

Madame Fournier [*piano tutor*] came for me in the morning, and in the afternoon Maudey and I went to the Beaumont grounds again to sketch, where Bess and Cis turned up, who had been shopping. While we were there, the regiment came through Bizanos by the new road, the band playing lovelily, to which we listened with pleased senses. We stood - or rather, I stood - till the sunset made everything look mauve and gold and my eyes drank it in eagerly, but at last, not wishing to go along the streets in the dark, I came home with regret, leaving however my parasol behind me, which I had to go back for. I did not leave it on purpose, though it sounds like it. Everybody stayed at home in the evening and Crispin Ken [*a recent 'sensation novel' by Rev. Arthur Robins*] went on rapidly, though a more miserably melancholy book I've never read, I think.

Pau, Saturday, February 1, 1862

Emmie came in the morning to scold us for having complained of her never coming to tea, which we denied having said. She asked Maudey to come to Perpignan with them in the afternoon, which she did. Mama, Jin and I went to the Bastarreches, Mama only however went in and we drove meanwhile to leave cards on the Alexanders, then we picked up Mama again and went to the Congreves but they were out, then to the Elisha Biggs. I stayed in the carriage and watched the children who were playing with their dogs in the garden. A small boy came up to me, saying, "Don't you intend to go upstairs?" No, says I. "Perhaps you don't know Mama." No, I don't, says I, on which the small boy ran away. After the Biggs, we went to the Montebellos, where we stayed ages. I had Marie and Evelyn to talk to. Finally, after leaving Mama at Mrs Martins, we came home, where we found a note from Kate on the table saying that Harry did not care to go to the Pen and Pencil Club meeting, would any of us go instead? So off set Jin and me to find Kate and tell her that Bess would go. She was still out, but we waited for her and she appeared in time, Harry and all, to whom I talked and who accompanied us back home to carry the "Christy Minstrels" [*books of sheet music?*]. Bess went with Kate, and Maude with Miss Macgregor to the club in the evening. At Mrs Hudson's there were some very clever things written, and at the end was a charade, the word acted being 'pillow'. Mr Pakenham, Mr Brydon, Captain Alcock, Mrs Alcock, and Mrs Grogan and Mrs Philpotts acted, and capital it was. We sat up till they came home to hear the account, and to give the account of a mess we had got into during the evening.

Pau, February 2, Sunday

We got up early to go to the early service which was done by Mr Ogle and Mr Hattersley. We had soon to set out again for the morning service, and we disliked very much having to walk out with everybody nearby looking at us. We also went to the French service to hear Mr Froissart who preached for the Cauterets church a very good service on charity. Bess, Cis and I also remained for the afternoon service, so we had six hours of church during the day. Mr Hedges was too ill to appear, so other people shared it between them. I slept all the evening.

Pau, February 3, Monday

I sketched from my window, and read Kingsley's Miscellanies in the morning and also went out with Caroline and Jin to the park where we walked and talked of nothings and came home again gladly. In the afternoon, Jin and I went through Gelos to the bottom of the Montebello chateaux, where we rested and finally turned homewards again, and how delicious was an armchair after our fatigues. Bess and Maude had walked with little Power. In the evening we first read Bessies and my donkeys [?] and then Crispin Kerr, which I do truly dislike. Mama was present at the donkey reading.

Pau, February 4, Tuesday

Read and worked and went with Mama in the afternoon, first to the Powers where Mama saw Miss Power, then to the Story's to see the things for the lottery. I went with Amelia into her room, but the Miss Ormsbys were there too, which was a bore. We met heaps of people on the stairs coming up, and saw everybody nearly while we were out. Talked to the Turners who were standing in a carriage before the Hepburns door, and who said they arrived on Friday. Bess drove with the Packenhams. Mama and Jin went in the evening to the Holders and we four stayed snugly at home and I worked. I practised my first little song, such a dear little fellow in the minor. I do like him so much.

Pau, February 5, Wednesday

The sweetest of sunniest days. I read, worked and went to church in the morning. The Alexanders came to hunt us out for a walk, so Jin and I went with them in the afternoon. Monsieur Bastard walked with us as far as the Basses Plantes where we were to meet, and tried to impress upon me the duty of talking French whenever I had an opportunity. We talked to Captain Story and Miss Hewitt for some time, then walked to Biltère, and through a wood where there were some scrambly places to get over, which Constance couldn't possibly manage to do by herself, so I had to pull her over them. When we took them home, I went up to her room, a little poky den like a maid's, all dirty looking and not very agreeable to breathe in, though the window was open. We got the club rules to study. I began to practise when I came home, but Mr and Mrs Fitzgerald came in, notwithstanding being told that I was the sole occupant of the house, and I had to entertain them all alone; then Mama brought in Mrs and Kate Costobadie who stayed to tea, but my pate was very empty, and I didn't know of anything to say, so I must have been a stupid companion. Mama, Bess and Cis went to the Bastarreches in the evening. It was such a crowd that nobody hardly could dance. Mr Packenham had strained his back out hunting so mama chaperoned Caroline.

Pau, February 6, Thursday

I finished trimming my frock in the morning. Mr Packenham called, but I missed him. The Congreaves asked some of us to go to croquet, so Jin and Bess went and had a jolly game. Mama and I went to a lottery for orphan children, where mama gained a case which contained a red velvet purse, notebook and mass book. Little Ormsby sat beside me for a long time, and I had rather fun teazing him till he came out with, "It wasn't Cis" that he asked to dance at the Bastarreches, upon which I told him that I wouldn't speak to him anymore. He asked me some question to see if I would keep my word, and when I didn't answer him, he ran away to his dancing master. The others went to the Spencers in the evening, where Little Ormsby declared he would go when he heard we were going, though I tried all I could not to let him. Howbeit, when the time came he never appeared. Mr Hodgeson was there and bored Bess to no end, and altogether it was not quite so nice as usual.

Pau, February 7, Friday

The clouds wept all day long, a fitting employment for we heard from Jack to say he was not coming at least for a long time. Oh, thee sad fate of our airy castles which now lie shattered in the dust. Hope on hope ever he may turn up in time. Work, work, work at Bessie's gown was our employment as Heloise is ill. Madame Fournier came to me and I read Kingsley and German, practised, sang and drew, not to speak of wasting my time at intervals. The Packenhams set off for the mountains. I pity them. We began "Our English Home" in the evening.

Pau, February 8, Saturday

O so cold! My journal feels, when my hand touches him, as if covered by a coating of ice. The cold kept most of us indoors feeling coddly [as in 'coddle', I assume] inclined. In the morning I read Kingsley, German, and worked for Bess; practised in the afternoon. The Thomases, Stephensons and Helen Holder called. Nothing occurred worth recording. I've resolved to do Constance some Sunday but how, is the question.

This was the first example of a code being used in the journal - quite simple to decipher, but what it means, and why it is encoded, I don't know. Perhaps Octavia was planning nothing more sensational than to paint Constance's portrait.

Pau, Sunday, February 9, 1862

More freezing than ever, and such biting winds as met our poor noses going to church. We had Mr Ogle and Mr Hedges in the morning, Mr Isaac and Mr Hedges in the afternoon. Very few people were out of mourning [for Prince Albert, presumably, who died 14th December 1861] only Mrs Cookson and that set, so we were glad we stayed in. There seems to have come a new importation of the masculine gender, for a lot of new faces appeared. I slept at every spare minute all day and the whole of the evening. When we went to bed, happening to cast a glance out of the window, a white world appeared, which accounted for the cold. The snow looks about 3 inches thick and certainly improves the beauty of our chicken yard, so I hope he'll remain there till I sketch him tomorrow.

Pau, February 10, Monday

As cold as ever, but today we go out of mourning, so I can henceforth wear my huge cloak which I did today, and very comfortable I found it. In the morning I sewed strings on my gown, but nothing else, time having set off in a canter. I walked with Cis in the park, it being the only practicable place. The Packenhams came and asked us to come to tea, which we did, except poor Bess who had to stay in to entertain Mrs Fitzgerald who would wait till Mama should come in. Miss MacGregor was there too and it was very nice indeed. We sat round the fire and talked snugly and settled that Emmie was to come over to us when the others next went out to a party. Mama, Bess and Cis went to the Hepburns and looked very jolly, having come out of mourning and being able to wear blue. Nevertheless, having a pretty dress did not make Cis dance, which was a bore. Bess stayed for some of the cotillon and came home with Mrs Stewart. I wrote to Eve.

Pau, February 11, Tuesday

In the morning I finished my letter to Evelyn and read Kingsley. In the afternoon I went with Maude and Jin to Miss Hay and Miss Spencer, then with Cis to Mrs Martin's where we found Lady Grey and the de la Poers. As soon as they were gone, in came the Packenham's and told us that Emmie was at home alone. Soon after they were gone Mr Chandless came, so we went away and walked for a little bit on the Jurançon road, then thought we should like to visit Emmie as she was alone, so back we went full tilt and were very snug in a lump on the floor before the fire until the other people came, soon followed by Miss Hewitt who in her turn was followed by Bess coming to bring them in to tea. Caroline said she couldn't come so we carried off Emmie and Miss Hewitt and had a pleasant time of it, only I'm sure Emmie didn't like me for some reason or other. In the evening Jin and Cis went to the Fournaises and enjoyed it very much, though it was a greater crowd even than the Bastarreches. They danced a good deal, which was satisfactory.

Pau, February 12, Wednesday

I finished altering my cloak, read Kingsley, went to church where we had singing, and we stood up and began singing when the organ was playing the prelude verse, and had to sink down ashamed. In the afternoon Jin, Bess and I went the round of Biltère across the Haute Plante where we met Constance who asked to come with us, and came out on the Bayonne road. I don't see any chance of doing Constance on Sunday, as they evidently want to get off a walk on that day, so I must try sometime else. This evening we were all at home and I did a habit-shirt for Pussie, as I had no work of my own. I began to write "Friends" but did not get very far.

Pau, February 13, Thursday

An unpleasant cold possesses me. In the morning I wrote friends and felt very unprofitable after it and read Kingsley. I went with Mama to the Powers of Biltère who were out (bless them for it) then home by the Bayonne road and had a good practise till the others came in accompanied by the Congreaves, and soon after appeared Miss Buchanan; a goodly assembly of females, not forgetting Emmie who came too. Florence stayed till late and I do like her. My cold stuffed up the door leading to my ideas, so I stood speechless like a stuck pig as I was and looked stupid. In the evening, Jin, Mama and Bess betook themselves to the Cliffes and we stayed snug downstairs till bedtime which for me came early, and tomorrow I'm to snore all day under my white covering or quilt.

Pau, February 14, Friday

The snoring process took place and very warm it was and comfortable, reminding me of my happy sick days. I read Kingsley and German and snoozed between whiles all the rest of the day, except the spaces left for thinking, which however did not occur often. Helen Holder came and excited a slight commotion in some people's minds by expressing a certain wish, the result of which remains to be proved. From my recumbent posture I watched the lengthening shadows on the opposite wall till my eyelids winked themselves to sleep and my head found a place on my pillow.

Pau, February 15, Saturday

I rose betimes, but made not a good use of the time gained. I read Kingsley and dawdled till luncheon, besides having a long practise as the others went out. After luncheon three of us went to Ellen's concert, two with the Countess Kalling, one with Mrs Packenham. The Spencers joined us and I sat next Ina, but was not very agreeable, my cold having still in its possession the key of the cupboard where my ideas are kept. Mr Congreave sung 3 things, Louisa playing his accompaniments. The last song was lovely and encored; the two first were sung out of tune. Miss Boscari played with the violins, and also a duet with another woman, very clearly but not from her inmost self. Her shakes [*vibrato?*] were lovely. In the middle Mrs Spencer went out and Ugh instead Mr Hodgeson came and squatted beside me, having previously been ensconced on the floor, a very good place for him. However, he found me not very gracious, so he went and sat where he would have a very good view of Maude, and made good use of his position. Coming out, he attacked me again, and with many he-he-hes hoped I had kept my health, etc., etc., etc. I carried Ina home with me and settled to walk with her next Tuesday. She read my Pen and Pencil Club things and estimated them far above their worth. I showed her my room and kissed her at parting, for I do like her. She told me that Amelia Story had far from a pleasant life of it. Poor child, I do pity her.

Pau, February 16, Sunday

Rain was our companion going to church. Mr Thursby, the red man's brother [*possibly a reference to the Improved Order of Red Men, a fraternity in the USA*] did the service and I liked him very much. He read fast and rather high toned, a pleasing variety. Between the services, Jin and Maude walked with the Packenhams. I was not allowed to go to church the second time, so I read Culture and Discipline of the Mind [*by John Abercrombie*] and did various things. We had music in the evening and no letters. What are my correspondents thinking of?

Pau, February 17, Monday

In the morning I practised, read Kingsley and cut out collar and sleeves. The Packenhams came to ask Cat and Cis to drive with them, which they enjoyed greatly. Jin, Bess, I and Mama went down to the croquet, but found nobody there, so had a game to ourselves. Then Mr Anderson came down and joined us with his dog Chip. It was very hot, and we were very tired and don't intend to go again without a made up party, as we found it stupid. In the evening, Mama and Jin went to dine at the Marchant Thomases, and we four had dinner solo and had a long old maid's gossip after it planning a picnic etc. Emmie came at 8-30, and we amused ourselves blacking our eyebrows and making ourselves moustaches and imperials; then Bess did a ghost and Maude and Emmie did scenes and Emmie had a music lesson. Bess and Cis went to an after-dinner dance at the Stewarts. Danced a great deal and liked it immensely; Little Stewart was doing duty all the time, good little boy.

Pau, February 18, Tuesday

Read Kingsley, practised and worked. Colonel Spencer asked some of us to ride, but we could get no horses, though we hunted all over for some, so had to give it up with great regret as we longed to go, it being a glorious day. Mrs Bacon took Jin driving to Morlaás to sketch. The Packenhams took Maudey driving, Bess and Cis went violetting and I walked with Ina Spencer along by the nice river beyond Bizanos where we came upon Captain Mowbray sketching. We sat down a little further on, and while Johnny was engaged in making a hocquet stick I had a nice little bit of good talk, but I was not eloquent and we were soon disturbed by the said Johnny who had lost his ball and wanted us to look for it. Then we went on our way and were much astonished at meeting the Hepburns. We spoke to them, and a little further on we found the little bride and her husband sitting by the river reading a book together. On we proceeded and sat down for a bit to rest. On getting up again, we saw Lady Katherine Parker coming towards us, so we talked to them and at last came home rather tired. Mama dined at the Fitzgerald's and Jin and Maude went up in the evening, but it was neither amusing nor stupid. I began a letter to Miss Obach and as usual went to bed.

Pau, February 19, Wednesday

Oh dear! Why cannot I get up in decent time??? I was late for prayers in consequence. You lazy pig! We went to church - what should one do without it? - and I worked all the morning. In the afternoon, Jin and I went in and out about Jurançon and sketched, staying out very late. We heard last night that little Livy was very ill indeed again. I read German and Monthly Packet [*The Monthly Packet of Evening Readings for Younger Members of the English Church*] all the evening. Mama, Bess and Cis went to the Hudsons. Cis liked it very much and danced enough though it was immensely crowded.

Pau, February 20, Thursday

Saved my character by tumbling up betimes, yet was late for prayers and pricked for it. I read Kinglsy and drew, practised and read the tract on light [*surely not the work on optics by George Biddell Airy*]. Colonel Spencer offered to take the girls out riding, only one horse could be found so Maudey rode. Cis and I went to get Rose Spencer for a walk, and found there Mr Somerset who asked if he might come too. Accordingly, we walked all about Biltère looking for violets, of which we found 7. Looked into the church and must have greatly disturbed a poor priest who was there. Met Mr Packenham and Emmie and talked for a bit, went into the churchyard, and at last carried Rose home with us to tea. Showed her all over the rooms, and I liked her myself. In the evening the others went to the Swinburnes, which Bess enjoyed very much. Not quite so much did Cis, for though she danced much, yet it was with stupid people.

Pau, February 21, Friday

Late again. In the middle of my dressing I got a letter from Evelyn which I gloated over, but she is not right yet and was very odd. Hope on hope ever. I read Kinglsey, practised and had Madame Fournier who gave me 10 tickets for her concert to dispose of, much against my will. In the afternoon, Cis and I sat in the Beaumont grounds, she reading, I finishing a sketch. We watched with great interest a kite going up and a small boy paddling through the river. etc. We were great babies, and laughed enough to serve for a week. Everything was very lovely and sunshiny, which sunshine found its way inside us too. Came home for tea, during which repast I thought I saw a piece of bread and butter on my gown, took it up on its way to my mouth, not taking any pains not to squeeze it, when I felt it move in my fingers and it curled itself up. I dropped it with a squeak and found it to be a sleek fat caterpillar, a near relation of Mr Slug. It finally was spooned out of the window by Cis, I daresay not feeling much better for the squeeze. Nobody went out tonight for a wonder, so Mama went very early to bed. I sat over the fire and read "Association of Ideas". Finally to bed.

Pau, February 22, Saturday

I read Kingsley, drew and practised in the morning. Bess rode with Mr Fitzgerald and Mr Cliffe. We all went to Perpignan, Jin and I walking by the riding way, and feeling like a repetition of the mountains we went to the anemone field, but the field was bare so we poor fellows got none. Next we went down a road hoping to sketch, in vain, however we got some violets for our pains and came all five in the carriage until the bottom of the hill when Maude and Cis got out and walked home. In the evening we went on with "English at Home" [*a novel by Constantine Henry Phipps, Marquis of Normanby*] and I finished a pair of cuffs. We got a letter from Miss Steele telling us that little Livy was taken home on the 19th, happy little thing, one cannot feel sorry.

Pau, February 23, Sunday

A new parson preached both morning and afternoon for the Church Missionaries. The HC [*Holy Communion*] was given out. In the afternoon a fresh girl sat before us with plats of which I never saw the like. Each plat was 3 inches across, simply platted in 3 plats just like huge cables, and it must have been long enough to sit on. I kept company with my room most of the day and slept in the evening. Mama says she will refuse all the coming parties and subside for a bit.

Pau, February 24, Monday

Wrote to Evelyn and not much else in the morning. I went with Mama to the Alées in the afternoon where we sat. The little bride and her husband were pacing up and down behind us. At last the Packenhams' carriage came, and on seeing us they got out. I had Caroline, Mama had Mrs and they took us in the carriage to Helen Holder's, where I played with Agnes in the garden till Miss Hepburn came and we went home. Emmie came to tea and stayed till late. The evening was passed at home.

Pau, February 25, Tuesday

Read Kingsley and finished my letter to Evelyn over which I took much trouble, it being rather hard to write. We were to have ridden with the Fitzgeralds but the rain stopped us. We went up to ask about it. Finally it cleared, so the others went out and I stayed at home solo to practise and write to Lily, in middle of which Caroline came, stayed for tea and went away late. Again no letters.

Pau, February 26, Wednesday

I read Kingsley and wrote and worked and went to Church. Miss Smyth's wedding took place which Jin and Cis said the bride looked very pretty. There were 8 bridesmaids who did not look their best, and the happy pair went to Argelès for the honeymoon. Bess and I rode out with Mr Fitzgerald, and my hand is so stiff and shaky I can hardly write. Bessie's steed was not as good as might be. We went round through Jurançon to the Lescar suspension bridge and came home by the Bayonne Road. My hair all came down and we had to stop twice to stick it up. Nevertheless, I went through the town with it streaking down my back. Miss Buchanan came to tea and told how once she was shipwrecked.

Pau, February 27, Thursday

My bones are feeling rather rusty after yesterday's ride. In the morning I read Kingsley and wrote notes to lots of people to ask them to take my concert tickets, only one of which, the Spencers, did any good, and Mr Somerset came to fetch them but did not stay very long. Still I have five to dispose of! We four set off, intending to go to Gelos for violets, but Bess and Maude, having gone to the Powers first, took fright at seeing some tipsy men and didn't dare to go, especially as we heard that some tipsy conscripts had played leapfrog over an unfortunate old gentleman, and they were afraid of the same being done to them. Cis and I, however, went on wondering why the others didn't appear. I sketched the ones in the Gelos village and we got heaps of violets coming back, from the inside of an old woman's garden hedge. We began "Old Folks from Home" [or 'A Holiday in Ireland in 1861', by Mrs Alfred Gatty] in the evening, but I didn't care much for it myself.

Pau, February 28, Friday

The Alexanders called in the morning, and Emmie. Madame Fournier came in the middle of them on which they retreated to Bessie's room. Maude and Cis rode with Mr Fitzgerald; Mama took the rest of us in a carriage as far as Place Gramont from whence Bess and Jin walked, and Rose and Mr Somerset came in the carriage down to the plain where we found the Packenhams already arrived. It was ages before we could begin the game as they were so long bringing down the things. Emmie, Bess, Mr Somerset and I were on one side, Caroline, Jin and Rose with two balls on the other and a hearty fight we had, but I'm sorry to say the enemy gained it. The Packenhams had to go in the middle, but we went on without them and were as spiteful and malicious as we could be, roqueting each other away without mercy. Bess and I walked up and joined Ina Spencer for a bit, the others went home carriage-wise and all came to tea, during which we had great fun. They looked at all our photographs and went home at 6, agreeing to meet again on Monday for a pitched battle on the plain.

Pau, March 1, Saturday

Finished my letter to Lily and read Kingsley. Taldoni [*publisher and singing instructor*] came for the first time to me and I howled for

20 minutes (alias sang) and he was not cross. Amelia came to go with me to the Spencers, who were to chaperone us to Madame Fournier's concert. We got to the front row which was not as nice a place as might be, beside the Ottleys. The concert was splendid. Mr Bazzini [*Antonio Bazzini (1818-97), violinist, composer and friend of Paganini*] played on the violin in a way to make one creep, which is not usual with a violin. O it was lovely! Madame F. played Home Sweet Home and an old man sang comic songs with a fat bass voice very well. Rivares, Becker and others played in one thing, but all out of tune which seemed greatly to bore Mr Bazzini who played at the same time. Maude and Cis had gone with Mrs Le Marchant-Thomas and sat in the same row with the Rose Spencers. After the concert, Amelia, Ina and I went to the Beaumont's grounds and sprawled under a tree. I felt dreadfully ancient beside the other two who kept pushing and bumping each other and laughing at nothing, just like Cis and me 3 years ago. Amelia stayed to tea and went home at 6. I got a letter from Tom in the evening at last but I didn't like it, it seemed as if he thought I should care for nothing but common things.

Pau, March 2, Sunday

Mr Isaac and Mr Hedges shared the morning service. We stayed for the HC. Between the services we went with the Packenhams to the Beaumont's grounds. Maude had Emmie, Bess had Caroline and I sat under a laurel bush by myself and enjoyed it much. A deacon did the service in the afternoon very well, and Mr Hedges sermonized; very good ones both times. I had a slight headache all day which crescendoed in the evening and was a bore. Sitting over the fire before dinner Cis, Bess and I had a snuggish talk on things to be hereafter. I slept all the evening and went to bed early.

Pau, March 3, Monday

Read Kingsley, sang and drew. The others were to go to croquet, but it rained, so instead they fetched Rose and Emmie here and we played hide and seek, les graces [*Le Jeu des Graces*] ball and battledore till 4 when Ina came to walk with me. We went to the very end of the park and back and were caught in the rain. Ina would take me home, so I kept her to tea and to be dried as her cloak was well soaked. The Baby came to be played with and was very amiable to Emmie whose heart it quite won. I finished a pair of sleeves in the evening as Cis read.

Pau, March 4, Tuesday

Shrove Tuesday, with its necessary accompaniments of pancakes and procession. In the morning I read Kingsley and worked. We had luncheon at 1 and at about 1/4 to 2 the procession came in sight. Alice, Constance, Miss Hichins and Miss Holt and the Packenhams came to see it. There were no Frenchmen that we knew, though we had seen Mr Bussel on his balcony in a grand Spanish dress, however he didn't appear. There was an odious figure of Bacchus sitting on a cask with a bottle up to his mouth and horribly painted, and the band in a car drawn by 6 horses. Jane Congreve came just when it was all over. We five then went out together to get violets from Gelos and got a good quantity, though at the expense of a squabble. We had dinner at 5, for the others were going to a lecture given by the little baron at Mrs Mitchell's, which spoke greatly of revivals. Two other men besides the baron spoke and that's all I heard about it as Cis and I stayed at home. I slept over the fire, read and worked and had tea when the others came home. I hope to get up at 7 tomorrow.

Pau, March 5, Ash Wednesday

Went to Church and worked. Taldoni came for the 2nd time but the Spencers arriving to see the carnival, I declared that I couldn't sing when they were there, so he went away. We had a lot of people to see it: Weekses, Sir Thomas Hepburn, Mary and Amy, Lady Louisa, Constance and some small fellows, the whole family of old Spencers, Mr Somerset and Rose, Mr Gough, Mr Marchant-Thomas, Mr Lagotellerie, Mr De La Poer. We got a supply of maize, though it was forbidden to pelt, and the police came upstairs and put down Mr Somerset's name to frighten us, but we were so civil that they let us pelt ever after. Little Fanny Power came too. We got heaps of bouquets thrown in to us which we threw at any nice people. The Morleys and Colonel Coryton and Amelia Story were also of the party, I forgot to say. Mr Somerset gave Mama his photograph, rather a good one. We had a grand array of eatables which speedily disappeared and Mr De La Poer and the Rose Spencers stayed till 6, at which period we came to the conclusion that we were very tired. We settled to go to croquet tomorrow with the Spencers and little Fanny Power. We finished Mrs Gatty in the evening and heard that old Rosey is going to be married!! at which Jin rejoices not.

Pau, March 6, Thursday

I finished a sketch and a collar while Mr Bazzini was fiddling with Maude. I tried to read but found the attempt useless, for they were playing the most lovely thing and made my feelings quite excited. It could not the least be compared to angels' music as some people compare a lovely concord of sounds, but it suited so exactly the longings, passions and sadnesses of us little piquises that it pricked one like a pin. My pen shall be sentimental no more. In the afternoon I rode with the Spencers. Bess had intended to go too, but her horse abandoned her. There was also a Colonel Templeton whom I had seen before in Church and to whom I had taken a great dislike. We went through the Bizanos wood and round by Caesar's Camp, coming back by t'other coteau. Mine was a jolly horse, and if it had not been for an uncomfortable saddle the ride was delicious. The others (Mama and Cis and Bess) went to an evening concert at the Bastarreches. Maudey played the delicious thing over to me while I read Kingsley, which I have nearly finished, and Longfellow took its place. A letter from Tia in the evening.

Pau, March 7, Friday

Nice and stiff am I after my ride. Sketched, read and went to church and had Madame Fournier. Mama and I went calling in the afternoon to Mrs Martin (out) Bacons (in) Lady Louisa (out) Foxes (in) Mansfields (in). At the Alexanders Mama wanted to settle her bonnet, so she was shown into Mr Alexander's dressing-room at which I was in a great fright lest he should come in and catch us. Maude and Cis walked with Florence and brought her into tea. Jin and Bess brought Rose from croquet and Caroline also appeared. The Hewitts came for 5 minutes and asked Cis to go to a picnic tomorrow which was accepted. We began David Copperfield in the evening.

Pau, March 8, Saturday

Taldoni came to me and Bazzini to Maude. Cis went off to a picnic at Biltère with the Hewitts, Alexanders, Packenham, Congreaves, Harboards, Captain Story and Captain Stracy and had great fun, though some of the party were too wild. Bess and I went down to croquet with Mr Somerset, who had got a wretched *coup de soleil* headache. Rose Spencer, Lena and Florence went down with Mama in a carriage. It was immensely windy and showery and twice we took refuge in a cottage during which we amused ourselves making jokes and playing How, When and Where. Our hats took to going home, so they gave Mr Somerset many a good chase. I was on Rose's and Florence's side and played very badly and lost the game. Coming up again we 5 girls squeezed inside the carriage and Mr Somerset on the box. We adjourned to the Foxes to tea and Mr Alexander came in afterwards, so we made him sing, then Bess, Florence and Lena sang in turn. Happily I had not to play. I did like Mr Somerset today so much, particularly while Florence was singing the "Bridge" and altogether he was very nice today. Mr Alexander walked home with Bess and me and settled to come and sing on Monday. In the evening Maude and Cis went to the Marchant Thomases. Going to the picnic, Cis had Alice Alexander to herself and made good use of her time. Maude also took a great fancy to Evelyn Montebello, for she was nice. I wonder if in after years I shall be able to recollect the meaning of all the mysterious little sentences I put in. I do hope I shall [*a reference to various coded passages, some of which I have deciphered*].

Pau, March 9, Sunday

I forgot to mention the subject which is in everybody's mouth, namely the arrest of the young men. There had been a dinner at the Club on Friday night at which too much wine was provided. Going home, Mr Biggs, March, Hutton, Freddy, Hepburn, and de la Poer were walking near the Cordelier St when they met little Dugan. The good cheer had made Mr March affectionate, so he went up, put his arms round Dugan's neck and hugged him like a bear. Little Dugan did not respond to this embrace and called the gendarmes. A fight began. Mr March cut and hid; the gendarmes were thrown down and their swords thrown away. The end of it was that these gentlemen slept that night in the prison. Freddy somehow was let out and set off instantly for Biarritz, but was recaptured and marched back again this morning. Their sentence most likely will be three months imprisonment. Fancy a cousin of ours doing such a thing from tipsiness. Ugh! How odious! Bess and Cis have made the resolution never to dance with these people again, indeed they won't have a chance if 3 months is the period of time agreed upon. We went to Church. Mr Hedges preached a good sermon if he had not brought in the "dance of death". The others walked with the Packenhams and Cis with Kate. Mr Ogle preached in the afternoon and we had music in the evening.

Pau, March 10, Monday

Rain, rain, go to Spain might have been our wish today. I began Vaughan's History of England, sang, and finished my sketch down the street. In the afternoon Bess, Cis and I went armed with battledores to the Foxes and played and talked till 5. Mr Cecil and Miss Coryton came in too. While we were making the best of our way home, I suddenly heard my name and looking round found Mr Somerset who walked with us home and asked us to join a riding party next Thursday. We found Mr Alexander come to sing the duets with Bess, and also a bevy of girls ensconced in Maude's room, namely Emmie, Caroline, Miss Hewitt, Rose and Jane Congreave who turned into the drawing-room for tea, and did not add to the happiness of the singers, but at last they went and we settled to see the Congreves tomorrow, either with them or us. Cis was then made to sing, during which she was in a tremendous fright but performed very well. In the evening came a letter from Jack in England, telling of his safe arrival and that he should set off for Pau about next Monday, poor boy. He is all right, I think.

Pau, March 11, Tuesday

Bazzini came in the morning and Mrs Fitzgerald came down to hear him. I read Vaughan and had Galos [*Victor Galos, artist*] for two hours. Maudey and I were to go to Mr Alexander's concert, so went to [*Rue de*] Cazalis to wait for Mrs Fox who never appeared. At last, after pacing the Halle for ages and hearing the concert going on above our heads most tantalizingly, we came home in despair. Mama was so sorry that we should miss it that she went with us instead, but it did not repay the walk, through the rain being very ugly indeed. We found Caroline here when we came back, and oh, how she bored us!! In the evening, Mama, Jin and Bess went to the Spencers. We others went to the Packenhams, where I was bored again nearly all the time except when I got near Emmie and my pity revived entirely.

Pau, March 12, Wednesday

Read Vaughan, practised, and Taldoni came but he was very cross indeed, which put me in a fright and sent my voice away. Jane Congreve and Emmie came in the afternoon as it was raining, and we played all our baby games. Bona and Ina came to tea. We are going to have some sort of a party on Friday and began asking people for it.

Pau, March 13, Thursday

Emmie came and painted here in the morning and heard Bazzini play. I painted all the morning. Mr Alexander came and sang with Bess, during which I took 3 portraits of him, none of which were like. He stayed to luncheon and then went away. He goes to Spain tomorrow, so we shan't have him to sing at our party. I stayed in and had a good practise, 2 hours and 1/2 in all, after which my fingers felt better. Some of the others got heaps of petticoat narcissus and other lovelinesses. Mr Packenham came back after seeing Freddy safe across the Spanish frontier, and Mr Hutton is to make the prison his habituation for 15 days. Young Hepburn and De La Poer for 8, also a fine is to be paid. They held a regular levee all day, heaps of people went to visit them and were received in the prison kitchen!!! I read Archbishops of Canterbury before dinner.

Pau, March 14, Friday

Emmie came and drew here. Madame Fournier came to me and as soon as she was done, Galos came and lasted till 4 when B, Jin and I sallied forth and prowled about the town. When we were coming in we happened to meet Jane Congreve with some other people, so forgetting that no tea was to be had I asked them in, and soon after they appeared, to my dismay when I found what I had done. Preparations for this evening were going on all day and at a little past nine people began to come. The room soon filled and the young ones turned out into the hall, leaving the old chaperones in the drawing-room. Music went on at intervals, some of which was greatly applauded by clapping, especially the glees and Christy Minstrels. At one time I made the tour of the drawing-room and doing the agreeable to everybody, at the end of which I asked them to take some tickets for Bazzini's concert; I succeeded pretty well and in all found places for 8 tickets. I had to play, so did L'Arabesque. I talked to nobody in particular, being most of the time solo behind the piano, which by the bye was moved into the hall. The people were all gone by 12 1/4 having enjoyed it, I believe. There was such a buzz that one need be in no fright whatever of being heard when one talked. I was much edified by a conversation between Bess and Mr Lagottellerie on sympathies and various suchlike topics, which really was worth listening to. Mr Somerset asked to come on a wet day to sing bass to our glees. What should we do without Three Blind Mice, which always has the effect we want it to have of making people laugh? The Rose Spencer party were left the last of anybody, so we gave 3 cheers twice over to Rose for having helped us out in the playing, she being the only creature besides ourselves that musicated. Emmie liked this party much, though she still said she preferred seeing her friends in the morning. Altogether it went off very well and I'm glad it is over. I'm very sleepy, so goodnight.

Pau, March 15, Saturday

Bazzini came and played o so lovelily. Emmie was here painting to listen to him, also Mrs Fitzgerald. I read "Archbishops" and Vaughan. Taldoni came and was not cross this time. Jin and I went to see after Kate why she didn't appear last night. She was out, but we stayed with the mother a long time. Home again we trotted and met the others going to see Miss Power, and soon after a note came in from the Packenhams telling us to go there and hear Hamilton read some of the Club things aloud. So Jin and I went and were much edified and amused. They asked me in particular to come. I wonder why? Mama went to the PPC [*Pen and Pencil Club*] meeting with Capt. Alcock in the evening. We passed that period chiefly in sleep.

Pau, March 16, Sunday

What did we do today? Even the same as every Sunday: two services, read, and slept all the evening. Maudey made a fierce onslaught on a little party between the services. Meanwhile, I amused myself most unprofitably drawing pretty girls' faces! - Cis got a letter from Gerty of an unsatisfactory nature.

Pau, March 17, Monday

I painted the whole morning. In the afternoon I went shopping with Cathy, and the others went down to croquet and had Cecil Fox, Rose, Fanny Power. The two last came home to tea. Caroline also appeared and bored us greatly. Heaps of people called today from time to time. We heard that Jack is to set off for Pau on today or tomorrow. How nice it will be to have him, won't it?

Pau, March 18, Tuesday

Galos came and I finished my picture and sketched another. The Alexanders came and Blanche sang with Bess not a particle in tune; how our poor ears might be pitied. In the afternoon, Jin, Cis and I went to get the petticoat narcissus but found very few. We tried to get Rose or the Alexanders but they had all gone out. An old Frenchman pulled us up a clay bank, and a good weight he must have found me to pull; active Jin had skipped up by herself. We then found some nice little mossy knolls where we ensconced ourselves at a good distance from each other. I sprawled on my back and gazed at the sky, examined a narcissus and meditated deeply. Suddenly I heard some voices coming down a road near me so I jumped up and found it to be Colonel Spencer, Mr Hodgson and Ina. We talked for some time and Mr Hodgson remarked, he-he, that Cis and I, he-he, bore the greatest resemblance to the babes in the wood, he-he, that he had ever seen. We then came home and set off again for to see Miss Power, leaving Lena and Florence at tea here. We found the Packenhams there but in time they departed. We looked at Miss Hudson's drawings - oh so pretty - and at Gussie's. I was dreadfully stupid and silent and everything nasty but I couldn't help it. They made us play, so L'Hirondelle came forth, but I don't think they liked my playing a bit. They liked Cis's and made her play two things. In the evening, Bess, Maude and I went to Emmie, which was nice. We talked and they played and I read, etc, and we came home at about 10. Going to bed ended all.

Pau, March 19, Wednesday

Got early up for a wonder and practised before breakfast. Lena and Florence came to hear Bazzini play and I believe liked it very much. Next came Church, and soon after Toldini who flattered himself that my voice was vastly improved under his tuition. I let him think so as it pleased him, but chuckled inwardly, knowing that I had to thank some porter which I had swallowed just before he came, to make my voice strong. In the afternoon, Bess and I rode with Mr Fitzgerald round by Guindalos and Gan. FT pelted all the way from Gan, so we came home at a gallop from that place with our faces all black with our veils and very lovely altogether. Caroline, Emmie and Rose came to tea, and as 7 drew on our hearts began to beat and many times were our heads popped out of the window looking for some signs of Jack, but none came, so I suppose tomorrow will witness his arrival. Cis got a letter from my little Eve, at which my eyes grew rather green. Why, I don't know. I wonder whether she's tired of me.

Pau, March 20, Thursday

Hurrah! Jack's arrived, but of that in its turn. I painted in the morning and then went to the Packenham's to look at Miss Hudson's drawings. Jin and I had their house to ourselves as they were gone to a grand picnic of 60 people at Coarraze, so we took our time. I sat in their garden reading all the afternoon and very lovely it was. Then I copied Miss Hudson's picture of the Eaux-Chaudes and finished up by going with Jin to the Frasers who we found at home. Towards 7 our hearts began to go pit-a-pat and not in vain for soon Jack was seen coming down the street, headed by François and some carpet bags. How happy we did feel to have him again it was quite pleasant it was. We worked and talked all the evening and Jack came at bedtime to see our rooms. How nice it is to write his name as being with us. Hip Hip Hip Hura-i-h.

Pau, March 21, Friday

Madame Fournier forgot me, so is to come on Monday. Instead I read Vaughan and Archbishops and painted. Galos came in the afternoon, and while we were busy, in walked Mr Somerset to sing the glees. Bess was out so they could not happen, but he stayed some time and was great fun. Soon after he departed, Col. Spencer came, but not for long. After the lesson, and Mrs Weekes having gone, she having come when we were getting ready, Jack, Maude, Cis and I sallied forth. Everybody did look astonished at Jack particularly, as Catty was taking his arm and he holding an umbrella over her like two moony parties. We went to the park and then for shelter to the Place Graumont arches, where we found Mrs Fox and Miss Buchanan and paced with them, and finally home to tea, during which meal Mr Somerset again appeared to ask about the concert, and blew us up for peaching (shocking slang) about Fanny Power and Cecil Fox. Emmie came here for a little bit but was frightened by Jack and ran away. Read aloud in the evening.

Pau, March 22, Saturday

Taldoni came and told me to prepare a first song. Bess and Maude went out riding with Jack. Jin, Cis and I down to croquet with Florence. We expected Rose but she never turned up. I played very badly, was very cross and I'm sure Florence took a great dislike to me. Jin and Cis went to the Marchant Thomases in the evening to a musical, at which Bazzini played most lovelily. I finished trimming my hat and went to bed very late in consequence. I do wonder what conclusion Jack has come to with regard to me, for his eyes are so often watching me in a most uncomfortable way for me, and yet he never says anything, but looks as grave as a judge and takes everything in. *

* *I have been unable to discover who Jack was. Octavia had three brothers, none of whom had Jack or John as their principal given-name, so maybe he was a cousin, as he is sometimes alone with Octavia or another of her sisters without the apparent need for a chaperone.*

Pau, March 23, Sunday

Mr Hedges must be ill, for he never appeared in Church at all. Mr Isaac, Mr Hattersley and Mr Ogle shared the two services between them. The latter did a lovely sermon in the afternoon. I went out with Caroline, but she would sit with the others, which did not increase their pleasure, but I suppose she was afraid of being attacked [*in the sense of being engaged in a challenging conversation*] again, for I could not get her away at any price. We had music in the evening.

Pau, March 24, Monday

Had Madame Fournier. Read Vaughan and painted. Mr Somerset came in the afternoon to see about croquet, so he, Bess and I went to get Fanny Power. He asked if he should follow us upstairs, like a good dog, but I replied that good dogs generally waited at the bottom for their masters, so he took up his station on the stairs till we came down again. There were enough people for croquet without me, so I came home and painted all the afternoon. Cis rode alone with Jack. In the evening, Bess and Maude went with the Frasers, and I with Mrs Rose Spencer to Bazzini's concert. We came in late, and the only seat I could get was among a lot of French people, but afterwards Mr Weekes changed places with me and I got beside Miss De Vaeux. Bazzini played lovelily, especially Marche Funebre [*Funeral March, by Chopin*] but there was a horrible woman of about 50, vulgar, hideous and affected, who sang with a loud scrakey voice. Her husband also sang, but he was better. I heard a very amusing conversation going on behind me. Two females were remarking Madame Fournier's eyebrows, and after wondering if they were painted, one came out with this little sentiment: "I do like eyebrows to be just like a little mouse's tail." Mr Packenham came to tea here to bid us goodbye, as he goes tomorrow. I'm sorry he's going.

Pau, March 25, Tuesday

Practised, and finished a picture with Mr Galos. I rode alone with Jack, first to the croquet ground and then all among brushwood and stones in the part beyond, near the river, having to ford many brooks. We then went near Lescar, through endless Biltère woods, and home at last. I should like to have talked something more than small talk, but I didn't know how. I played all I possess in pieces before dinner, and very badly I did it, having forgotten them all. Jack gave Bess a lovely photograph book, which she speedily furnished with photos. I sketched Jin in the evening, and Bess and Cis went to the Hudson's with Margaret Hay. Mama went to bed early, being turned wrong side up. Fancy, my 18th year begins in 4 days. How odd. I wonder what my mind has been doing all this year.

Pau, March 26, Wednesday

Painted, went to Church, and had Taldoni with whom I began my first little song. In the afternoon, Cis and I trudged off to the Bezanos wood amid dust and sun, which pretty well did for me. We got heaps of flowers and trespassed through the grounds. I was sorely puzzled coming back to think how I should get home, when behind came a carriage. A voice squealed at us to have a lift, which we accepted joyfully and accompanied the Thomases home. Caroline and Emmie came to tea, and after that Rose. The Packenhams, Rose and we are to go to Pieta tomorrow for a small picnic.

Pau, March 27, Thursday

Pouring rain. So much for our picnic. I drew and practised and went shopping with Bess. Nobody came to battledore in the afternoon, so we had a good game by ourselves, after which the others went to the Powers, but were bored at finding a lot of people there.

I did nothing all the evening.

Pau, March 28, Friday

I painted and practised and went to Church. Mr Walsh gave his lecture, which put Bess and Mama in a rage, it being a regular hit at the Romanists. Galos came, after which I went to the Beaumont grounds with my book and gloated over the loneliness there. Such lots of birds made themselves heard and everything was pretty. On coming back I went to the drawing-room, and to my astonishment found Cecil Fox reading the Cornhill [*The Cornhill Magazine*] and also Florence. I had to go at these creatures for ages, and at last they went away just before the others arrived. Cecil Fox had been to the croquet ground to wait for Fanny Power and the others, and when they did not come he came here hoping to catch her at tea, but was nicely sold as the others went to them instead. My small talk came sadly to an end. I do wish we could get a fresh importation sometimes.

Pau, March 29, Saturday

The last day of my being 16. I'm so sorry. What a very happy year this is to look back upon. A new one is about to begin, and puts one rather in a fright as to what one may be like this time next year. Taldoni came and was as cross as 2 sticks and made me scream much too hard to be comfortable to my voice. I do wish he would not choose me to vent his ill temper upon. I drew all the morning. Emmie, Rose and Mr Somerset came and did battledore as it rained, and sang glees. We then went in a troop to the Beaumont grounds and ran races in which I was left far behind. At dinner a glorious bouquet was brought to me from an anonymous creature. I wonder whether it comes from the same quarter as the brooch and locket. It was meant as a birthday present I should think. I wonder if it is from Jack. I read David Copperfield in the evening.

Pau, My Birthday, Sunday, March 30th, 1862

Again has March 30 come round and I am 17. 16 is past and with it many happy days. On coming into the drawing-room, Mama gave me a book of all the Cascades in the Pyrenees. After admiring it I caught sight of an interesting looking fat white box with 'Baby' written on top. Inside was a splendid desk from Jack, with every kind of thing for writing and so many dear little store-closets, in fact a complete beauty. How rich I be. We came out of mourning and went to Church in "Sunday garments glittering gay". I suppose Mr Hodges is still sick, for he did none of the services. Mr Yorke preached a beauty of a sermon which I liked having come on my birthday. Between the services I stayed in and began a letter to Evelyn using my new desk, and after Church I walked with Jin down the new road and up through the Beaumont. Jack was coming too, but he absconded, and Maude and Cis went together. I slept and read tracts in the evening.

Pau, March 31, Monday

Madame Fournier came, and I wrote to Evelyn. It rained, so I stayed in all day and read David Copperfield. In the evening we had a small party consisting of Alexanders, Packenhams, Rose Spencer, Mr Corbet, Thomas, Goff, Cooper, Fitzgeralds. It was terribly stupid till the middle, and so much so that I went to bed in despair, but towards the end it revived and the last end was better than the first. Indeed, the joviality increased so much that I heard the laughing even in my room, so out I came again and took part in it. We played games with which we had forfeits, one of which was very pleasant, ie to waltz round the room, so I had a jolly waltz with Mr Somerset, who by the bye dances remarkably well. Singing and playing went on, of the latter I had not to subscribe my share which did not afflict me. All the people were gone at about 1/4 past 12 when we had prayers and went to bed.

Pau, April 1, Tuesday

Galos came and I finished my skin picture, read Archbishops and finished David Copperfield. Jack, Jin, Bess, I, Fanny Power, Rose, and the Packenhams went down to croquet, Jin, Bess, me and Caroline on one side, t'others on t'other. They gained it. Mr Somerset came down in the middle, having been to the meet. We played another game, again very badly, which we could not finish. Some of us came up in the Packenham's carriage, me among others, but it was too late to get people to tea. Ina came yesterday to see me and I found that my bouquet was from her, so I expressed my humble gratitude and esteem, etc. I like Mr Somerset, he is a nice little boy. Cis rode with Jack in the morning and heaps of visitors came in the afternoon.

Pau, April 2, Wednesday

Read Archbishops, went to Church and had Taldoni, Mama being present to prevent him from being cross. Gussy and Fanny came in the morning, and the others walked with Fanny in the afternoon. She stayed to tea and was so happy that she stayed to dinner too, and we had a jolly evening until Lady Power walked in all of a sudden and carried her off home, and I'm afraid gave it her pretty sharp on the way. Jin and I went over the canal, but I was sorely grieved to find that our nightingale place was all cut down. I sat disconsolately on its ruins, namely a heap of sticks, and began The Woman in White, [*recently published 'sensation novel' by Wilkie Collins*] but found it not so exciting as I imagined. We want to have a picnic with the Powers tomorrow, so I hope the weather won't be cross.

Pau, April 3, Thursday

There is a fate against our having picnics, for here is tiresome Mr Rain again, pattering prosily down with his dark grey nightcap on. I painted, read "Woman in White" and sang. Bess, Cis and I went to tea at the Pakenhams where Bess took her first lesson in sewing, over which we had great fun. I played for a piece, for I was left to the tender mercies of Caroline at one time and thought that if I played I needn't talk, but I am forgetting all my music.

Pau, April 4, Friday

Went to Church, where rather an improved edition in the way of a lecture was given by Mr Isaacs. I read Archbishops. Galos came and I finished my water and cow picture. After that I went out riding. We picked up Florence and set off on the Eaux Bonnes road, then turned a long way down a lane by being not able to go on. We came back again and ran all over Jurançon. Fanny Power came to tea, and the Alexanders for a magpie's nest visit. We began The Pickwick Papers aloud in the evening. Really, I am reading so many books at a time that I have not time to finish any.

Pau, April 5, Saturday

Taldoni came. Read Archbishops and worked and practised. Major

Goff, Mr Goff and Mrs Corbet came to call, so Mama asked them to go with us to croquet. Cis and I went to try for Florence, but she being out we got Mr Somerset and sat in the Basses Plantes to wait for the other gentlemen. They soon appeared, minus Jack, on which we declared that we would not wait for them so we set off a pace and reached the plain a good time before our pursuers. We got Fanny Power, and Maudey came carriagewise, but just when we were thinking of beginning, Cecil Fox turned up and joined us, much to Fanny's disquiet. Major Goff, Mr Corbet, Cis and I were in one game which was fearfully slow. I played wretchedly, as we had the big balls, and we only did one game. Mr Somerset and Fanny came to tea and we bought a cup and saucer on purpose for Fanny on the road.

Pau, April 6, Sunday

In the morning we had Mr Hedges and a new parson. We received the H.C. I sat by myself in the Beaumont grounds and read till service time. Cis got a letter from Willie and we had music.

Pau, April 7, Monday

Read Woman in White, and Madame Fournier came. In the afternoon, Cis and I went down to croquet. We met Helen who took us down in her carriage. We went to get Rose and Mr Somerset, who gave Cis and me some dear little Bankzia roses (What a way of spelling it) which we affixed to our persons. It was the Pakenham's croquet party and they brought down Mrs Harboard, Miss Hewitt, Lena, Florence and her brother, the ugliest little wretch in existence, and Mr Cecil. Two games went on. In one, Emmie, Lena and I played against Mr Somerset, Miss Hewitt and Caroline. The latter two played horribly unfairly, pushing their balls about under their dresses which made me very cross indeed. They gained the game by happening to play in the wrong turn when I'm sure we should have got it if it had been done properly. We had tea to refresh us after our game, and then people began another which was a most exciting one and lasted till 20 to 7. Rose and I then set off at a gallop, but Jack came up saying that he was in a hurry to go to Helen Holder's and that he would go quick instead of me, so I fell back to join the others, when they squealed out that Jack and Rose ought not to be seen alone and I was to join them again, so off I set at full speed, but all I could do did not make me join them. I ran down the hills and panted and puffed but all in vain. At last I arrived at the Basses Plantes. It was getting fast dark and I did not like being there by myself at all, especially as lots of soldiers were going about. I kept rushing about in a cracked manner to avoid them, first up one path and then another and at one time tacked myself onto the tail of an old French couple. About 1/4 of an hour I went on in this way, and at last the others appeared at which I felt considerably relieved, for the darker it got the more soldiers appeared and my fright increased to a great extent. We found the others in the middle of dinner and were exhorted to be better in future. Pickwick proceeded.

Pau, April 8, Tuesday

Galos came and I began the hard tree picture. I then began my singing, when the Powers came in to get us to go with them to the Beaumont grounds, where we all went in a lump and sat till 1/2 past one. In the afternoon I went with Mama to the Alexanders, whom we met just going out, then to the park where we stopped all the time. I had no book, so my stay there was not enjoyable. After the park we went to the Powers and had Lady Power and Dick, who took care to plant himself far away from me so as not to have the bore of talking to me. A letter from Alfred in the evening, containing some new photos which I did not like as much as the other, so Jin gave me hers and took a new one instead, which she liked better.

Pau, April 9, Wednesday

Taldoni came. We went to Church, on the way to which I saw little Ormsby for the first time for ever so long. In the afternoon the Fitzgeralds took Jin and me to the French races. We came in so late that we only just came in for the steeple chase. There were lots of tumbles. They however were not near enough to look disagreeable. Mr Arden gained, but they declared that he was not the right weight, so he missed all the honour and glory of it. I got the Echos D'Italie for my songbook, and the songs seem pretty. Mama, Jack, Jin and Bess went to the Taylors in the evening. I, meanwhile, wrote to Lily and finished The Woman in White. There was no dancing, at which people were greatly bored. Bess had to sing, and they enjoyed it very much.

Pau, April 10, Thursday

All the others went off to a picnic got up by the Foxes at Biltère. Cis and I were left solitary. Helen Holder came and stayed so long that we came in late at the singing meeting. There was a chapter read and talked upon which was very nice, indeed just the revival sort of thing. Whether it was done by Mr Denham Smith I don't know, as we could not see his face. We had to go out before the end, which was not pleasant to do, to drive with Gussy Power. We drove till past 6 and it was very pleasant. We ran races coming home with another carriage and gained it. Jack, Cis and I went at 8 1/2 to hear the new band, which was lovely. It played imitating a siege, or something like it, first one part of the band played loud, and the other answered it as from a distance, then there came some guns and a bugle, then a march, etc. Our mouths got full of smoke. The only friends we saw were Kate and Cub Fox. I finished my letter to Lily.

Pau, April 11, Friday

Went to Church, and as Mr Walsh was to give the lecture this time, we came out before it. At 1/4 to 3 we set off for our picnic in the house above the Montebellos. We had the Powers, Packenhams, Corbets, W Spencer and Major Goff. We first went up a steep hill, Mr Somerset pulling up Fanny and me. We sat on the top for some time, but some thunder being heard in the distance Caroline was afraid of getting wet, so we came down. I ran down mountain-wise. Then we had Prisoners Base and football till the rain sent us in. We then had tea, and glorious fun it was. We had a little table apart from the rest, and the gentlemen would run away with all our nice cakes, so we had several amusing fights. Next we did hide and seek, but the floors were too slippery to run much. Jack, in coming full tilt, went bang against a wall and cut his forehead and under his eye rather badly. After that we had the band game, with forfeits, which was great fun. Everybody was quite at their ease, which was comfortable, and they all enjoyed it immensely. We fitted in the Packenham's carriage coming home, and altogether it went off very well indeed. In the evening I got a letter from Evelyn. I wish she would not think me such a piece of perfection, for she will be so disappointed when she sees me. Little goose, she looks up to me as if I was the wisest creature in the world and her good angel into the bargain.

ARTHUR C. VENTRESS

Pau, April 12, Saturday

Taldoni came, and then Galos, in the middle of which lesson the Corbets called and I then went off to the races with Mama, Jin and Bess. We were early, so got a good place beyond the stand, but had nobody nice near us to talk to. Before the races began, the gentlemen came and talked to us. In the first race, the horse little Smythe was on fell and broke its leg. We saw nothing nasty in the way of tumbles, and Mr Power got all the races nearly. The rain came down plentifully, and we had hard work to get ourselves covered. I expected to be very much excited, but au contraire. Jin was to have gone to the PPC in the evening, but she had a headache, so I went instead with Mama. It was at the Thomases. I got near Emmie and was much amused. Some of the writings on "adventure" were capital. Then acted the play of "injustice" over again and also "The Unwarrantable Intrusion" [*a one-act farce by John Maddison Morton (1811-1891)*]. Mr Hewes and Mr Brydon were the principal actors and did it beautifully. We just saved ourselves from being there on Sunday morning, coming home at 10 to 12.

There follows this cryptic passage which I have been unable to decipher.

Pau, April 13, Sunday

Raining again and freezing cold. Coming home from afternoon service we met Mr Somerset and Fanny Power, so we got them to come to tea. Mama bestowed one of Cicell's plates on Mr Somerset, much to her horror, so they had a fight for it. After tea we had sacred music, in the middle of which Mr Somerset had to go, but Fanny stayed to the end. This little party promised me a photo of herself sometime. Little east wind gusts whistled through the inside of the house all day. I think I got out of bed the wrong side up.

Pau, April 14, Monday

Madame Fournier came and made me late for church. In the afternoon, Bess, I, Fanny, Rose and Mr Somerset went down to croquet. Rose and I played against the other three and beat them hollow. At least Rose did, not me, for I only just saved myself being called a bad player. We had great fun, and many jokes were perpetrated. I walked home with Rose, but only talked small talk, though it was such a good opportunity. They all came home to tea, where we found the Alexanders. They, however, soon departed. Jokes increased in number and it was very jolly. We likened ourselves to different animals. Maude was a cat and Jin a wren, Rose a Pau sheep, Cis a weasel, Bess a fat white rabbit, me a white mouse and Mr Somerset a vulture, snipe or hawk, we could not determine which he was to be. Fanny had had a fan sent to her in the morning from some gentleman without a beard, according to Gaupeau's account, so the only creature minus a beard that we could think of was Mr Somerset. I wonder whether it was him.

Pau, April 15, Tuesday

Galos came and kept Pussie and me from Church. In the afternoon we had a riding party consisting of Sir John and Fanny, Mr Somerset, Kate, Miss Tottenham, Jack, Bess and I. We first had a tearing gallop up the Allées, then got into the Sandes and somehow got to the path beyond Caesar's camp and home by the Bizanos coteau. It was a huge long ride and we were 3 hours and 1/2 doing it. Mr Somerset was at Fanny all the time, and Bess and I were two girls *de trop*, as some gentlemen had refused to come at the last minute. Florence and Emmie came to tea and Jack read Great Expectations aloud in the evening.

Pau, April 16, Wednesday

Taldoni came, and though not quite cross was superabundantly strict. We went to Church, and in the afternoon I went with Mama shopping and calling on the Steven--- Hays, where I talked to Miss Auchmuty all the time, and the Spencers who were out. Fanny came to tea.

Pau, April 17, Thursday

Went to Church and painted in the morning. We walked to Church with the Corbets and came in for a heap of gentlemen at the Club corner, by whom I was hemmed in on all sides, but at last squeezed happily through them. I went with Fanny and Maude to the meeting, where we arrived much too early, so prowled about till people came in. Mr Isaac did it all, as nobody came to help him. The Carpenters were there and looked amused at seeing us. At the end, Fanny introduced us to Miss Mahony, a dear pretty girl who shook our hands so warmly, saying that she knew us well by hearsay. We went to be talked to about Pierrefitte [*near Paris*] by Lady Power, and then sat with Gussy and heard her sing. It was so jolly. The Corbets came to tea. I should like Gussie to like me.

Pau, April 18, Good Friday

Went to both services, which Mr Isaacs and Mr Hedges shared between them. I went out with Walter [*brother, aged about 34*] between the services to the Bois St Louis, then behind the Beaumonts to get some Judas tree, and home by the dirty street. We talked a little moral, by which we cut shorter the way. The child belonging to the ropy-haired female was stuffed into our pew and amused herself studying our faces all service time. Fanny went with us to afternoon Church and then to tea. The Fortescues sent to ask us to their party, as Jack could not come, so Jin's desire is gratified as to knowing the Fortescues. Mama says I'm to go, as it is most for children. Whether I shall enjoy it remains to be proved, but I hope so to do.

Pau, April 19, Saturday

Taldoni came, and I painted. I was getting ready for Church when a note was brought me to say that Mrs Martin's carriage would call for me at 12, so accordingly it did and we all assembled at the Martins. There were the Gilbert Smiths, Ina, Amelia, Miss Ewin, Amy Hepburn, Fanny Hudson, Miss Hay and the Countess. We went to a house on the coteaux and hunted about for some shade which we at last found, and after dawdling about we ate, and they would throw spiders at me because I disliked them. Then we ran down a hill after oranges and sat in a wood playing games. I was tired after all this, so I came home in the carriage. The others all walked. We joined again at Mrs Martin's where we had tea, then all the girls played in turn. I played odiously, then to my horror they made me sing, though without any music or anything, but I think my song was not merry enough to please them. Next, the most discordant glees were sung that I ever heard, and they made me play the accompaniments though I had never played them before. Such a discordant noise as there was, such as I never wish to hear again. Finally we came home and well tired was I. Some of the others went in the evening to the Foxes to tea and I came early to bed, being headachy.

Pau, April 20, Easter Sunday

We went to the early service before breakfast. There was nearly everybody we knew there. I began a letter to Evelyn. How I wish she would send me the answer that I want. In the evening, all but Mama and Jin went over to the Packenhams. It was very dark and we all went and sat in the garden and sang. Then I paced up and down with Jack and talked good, but I don't know whether he liked it. We had tea there, which we would rather have missed, and came home. We had some more music at home, but we could not help laughing, at which Jack went to bed. We were sorry for that. I felt like the child's speech: "The world is hollow (except in a few little corners) and my doll is stuffed with bran", etc. We saw such lots of gloriousness in the Packenhams' garden. It reminded me of the mountains.

Pau, April 21, Monday.

Madame Fournier came and kept me from church, which I did not approve of at all. I went to get some new gloves to go to the Fortescues, and to pay for my bouquet where I found little Stewart and Dick Power bargaining about bouquets. Mama, Jin, Maude and I went to the Fortesques and I was fearfully bored, not to speak of my boots acting the part of a foot-screw all the time. There was a band on the balcony above the hall door which played dance tunes to which nobody danced, and people walked about and talked to their friends, but one couldn't get a comfortable talk with anybody, for gentlemen were sure to come and disturb one. Mr Somerset was devoted to Fanny, little Stewart to Gussy, and Mr Fox to Rose all the time, so that one could not get to speak to them at all. What bores men are. At last I went and sat by Miss Hay in despair. One time I thought I should have a jolly talk with Emmie in a tent there was, when a whole lot of people came and sat there too, much to my disgust. The people at home had a jolly ride. I wished

I was them. Croquet is settled for tomorrow. Oh how I do hate these small-talk parties where there is nothing but fine clothes and humbug. Ugh!

Pau, April 22, Tuesday

Galos came, and I practised and then finished Eve's letter. In the afternoon Jack, Jin and I went to croquet with Rose. Mr Somerset had settled to come, but he never turned up, and Fanny Power was tired so we 4 had it to ourselves. Jin and I gained the last of 3 games. I do so like Rose, for I think she likes me. There is to be a paper-hunt tomorrow, which Jack, Bess and I intend to ride to and see, where we shall meet Rose riding and lots of people. The prize is 400 francs, whereby Mr Somerset hopes to win Colonel Coryton's Ladybird [*presumably a horse*]. No ladies are to go, for many bad leaps are to be taken.

Pau, April 23, Wednesday

Taldoni came. Jin and Maude departed in state for the mountains at 8 1/4. I wish I was going too. We went to Church, and then shopped and met the Packenhams and walked home with them. In the afternoon Walter, Bess and I went to see the paper hunt. They met at the Allées. Only 6 gentlemen ran, among them Mr Somerset. I wonder whether he thinks I hate him, or what, for he never speaks to me now, which I'm sorry for as I like him. We saw a few leaps and followed as fast as we could. While I was galloping along, off came my hat and I had much work to stop my horse as he was sorry to miss his gallop, and while the unfortunate Jack was sent to fetch it, he amused himself going on as a dog does when his master comes to take him out walking - sweet little plunges and starts. However it amused him, I suppose, and I did not care much. Then off we set again and ended at the hippodrome, where lots of carriages were standing to see them come in. We stayed there a short time, and then went on to Lescar and got home somehow. Gussy came to tea and settled to start at 10 1/2 tomorrow, which made a mess, and Gussy found out that it was not liked. Fanny came afterwards; poor little pet, she did look so pale and harassed. I'm sure she's unhappy about something and I think I know what. Why cannot people be happy?

Pau, April 24, Thursday

At 10 o'clock Bess, Cis and Walter set off for the mountains. They took Fanny with them, and Mama and I were left the sole inhabitants of the house. I practised and sang nearly all of the morning. We had dinner at 2, after which I went to Miss Hitchens. Caroline came and stayed a short time. While we were at dinner the Montebellos called to bid us goodbye, as they are going away directly. Mama and I then went out in the carriage, first to Lady Powers, where I stayed in the carriage and covered myself up in my parasol to escape the eyes of the Club, then to sketch near Jurançon. We sent the carriage away and walked home, feeling more dusty at the end than when we set out. Mama went up to the Fitzgeralds in the evening. I sang Cicell's old songs and then wrote to Freideu's.

Pau, April 25, Friday

Emmie came over while we were at breakfast and asked me to drive with them, and also to come in the evening. She left me a lovely soup plate of roses on the table. I practised and painted and drove with the Packenhams. At 3 we went exploring and got out to walk. On the way we found the most delicious wood full of ferns and old owl-like trees and tiny green-arched lanes, and everything beautiful: a place where only happy people ought to go, and that were we. Then we walked up a hill and ended at Perpignan, the road beside the anemone vineyard. We got lots of seed and then drove back. I had a jolly bit of talk with Emmie before tea, which we had in the garden. Then I went home and found Jin and Maude come back from the Eaux Chaudes. Having visited all our pet places, I and Mama went back to dine with the Packenhams, and after dinner we went into the garden which was quite dark, and Emmie and I had another jolly talk. She's the easiest creature to talk to that I know. The others and Mrs Harboard came afterwards, and we came away in time very tired and sleepy.

Pau, April 26, Saturday

Taldoni came. I practised and painted, but it was so melting as to bring on an overwhelming fit of laziness, so not much was done by me today. I went out very little, but took up my station on Bessies bed and read, then leaned out of the window with Catty and talked and saw the Corbets coming home. There passed some wretched girls on huge stilts, who looked as if they had gone through a great deal before they could do it, poor things. It made me feel how happy one ought to be. Then the madman passed. It seemed to be one of his bad days, as he was shaking his fists and beating his breast and talking to himself. He looked so wild I should not have liked to have met him.

Pau, April 27, Sunday

We had a lot of room in our pew today, which was comfortable, the others being away, and comfort is necessary to keep one's attention fixed. I went to the Beaumont grounds and sprawled there by myself. The others were with Emmie. A jolly letter came from Bess, giving the account of an expedition to Cauterets and the Lac de Gaube, and seeing our dear old places. I began 'Life Work' in the evening.

Pau, April 28, Monday

Got up feeling awfully seedy and jaundice-like. Taldoni came, then Madame Fournier. I sketched the drawing-room and read Life Work. Maudey and I went to the Packenhams and stayed some time, as they go to the mountains tomorrow with Rose. Alice and Constance came to see us as they go tomorrow to Madrid, and Rose came too. Then we went out to the Mansfields and Mrs Spencer, and to see Blanche, who was squeamish, so couldn't come to us. We heard that Jack, Bess and Cis had gone to the Eaux-Bonnes. All the others, except 2 gentlemen, had come here today and were to set out again tomorrow for the Eaux. I do wish I knew whether I should go to the mountains after all, or not. Mama seems longing to go if it were not for the money. Maybe if I keep seedy she'll go. Oh I do hope she will.

Pau, April 29, Tuesday

Galos came, then I practised and sang. In the afternoon Miss Corbet drove Maude and me down to the plain, then went back to fetch the rest: Mrs Mansfield, Jin and the Goffs. Major Goff, Maude and I were against Mr Corbet, Mrs Mansfield and Jin. I played wretchedly at first, but when the others were sure of getting the game, fortune turned; I came up at double quick pace, scattered the enemy and brought in the friends. I was very pleased at thus saving my character. Then we had a race round the hoops, but people played so unfairly that we only made it a trial of in how many turns one could get through the hoops. We all walked home.

The Corbets, Goff and Mrs Spencer and the Countess Kalling came to a big tea at 8, at which we had great fun. Major Goff would cram my plate with everything on the table, etc. After tea, the Corbets played duets. I played and Maude too. We sang a glee, drew pigs, did puzzles and made jokes in abundance. It was very jolly, for one could do just what one liked and nobody was stiff. I wonder whether Major Goff thinks I'm a little girl of 12, very tall for my age. I do like Mrs Corbet so much.

Pau, April 30, Wednesday

Taldoni came. Next time will be my last lesson. I'm rather sorry, for I've got rather to like him, not having been cross for a long time. Went to Church where were only about 14 people, if so much. I practised and sang. The afternoon I spent by myself in the Beaumont grounds reading Life Work, and which I do like very much. Another letter came from the others at Eaux-Bonnes, still wild with delight, etc. Oh to go to the mountains. It would do me all the good in the world, for I feel horribly seedy.

Pau, May 1, Thursday

Mama was ill with pain in her side and headache so stayed in bed all the morning. I painted Maude, and I went to the singing meeting where we saw Miss Mahony whom we bid goodbye to as they go away next Wednesday. After that I went to Miss Hitchens and stayed a long time, I'm afraid, keeping her from her dinner, as I found the other people at it when I came out. I then read Life Work and sang.

Another almost unfathomable passage follows:

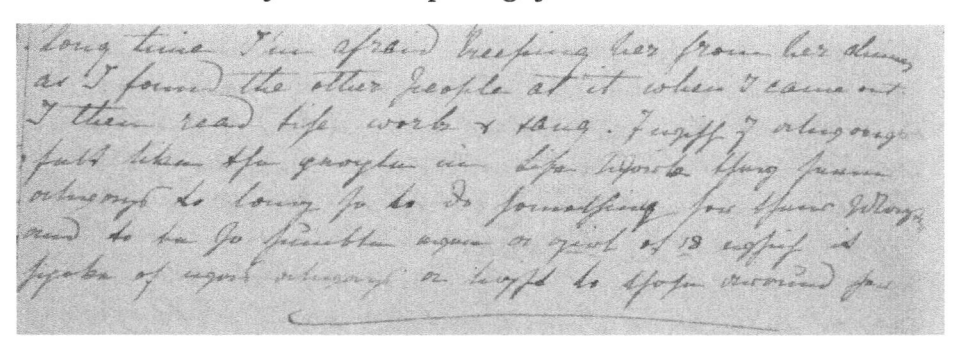

Pau, May 2, Friday

Taldoni and Galos came, old Tal for the last time. The Fitzgeralds came down while I was singing and made me sing to them after he was gone. Jin and I walked to the Congreves, whom we found at home, but a lot of people were there too. We had tea and walked home again, after which my feet were quite worn out with new boots, so I went and sat in the Packenham's garden and took them off and read Life Work. The others turned up from the mountains while dressing for tea and gave all the account all the evening, but as usual they had a lot of secrets to tell Puss, so I came to bed. I should like to hear and know what Cis knows and don't like being a little outcast at all, I don't.

Pau, May 3, Saturday

We went to find out what day we could be photographed, then to get some table covers. I read a good deal for a wonder. We went to the library, and I then came in and practised and sang all the afternoon. While I was thus squealing, somebody knocked gently at the door. Come in, says I, and in walked Mr Somerset. Poor boy, he does look so sick. I suppose it is with being in love. He wanted me to go on squealing, but I wouldn't, then he wanted me to play Il Bacio [*The Kiss, by Luigi Arditi, 1822-1903*] but I couldn't. Then we talked and he looked at photographs and took away his image. Going away he said, "Now can't you really play Il Bacio?" so seeing he did want it so much I did try to do it and got through it half by ear and half by music. I think he has got to like me again now, which I'm glad of. What a great many people there are in the world to be pitied, Mr Somerset among them, having fallen head over heels into an odd sort of pond called love, without a penny or the smallest shadow of hope, making himself ill thereby. Poor little boy. The Mansfields came and besieged us in the evening to enquire about Miss Obach, to whom I afterwards wrote. The others had gone to the Corbets.

Pau, May 4, Sunday

Went to Church and stayed. The Dean preached. A very nice man preached in the afternoon, and from his sermon I at last made out about [*a cryptic passage follows, which may be about Assyrians.*]

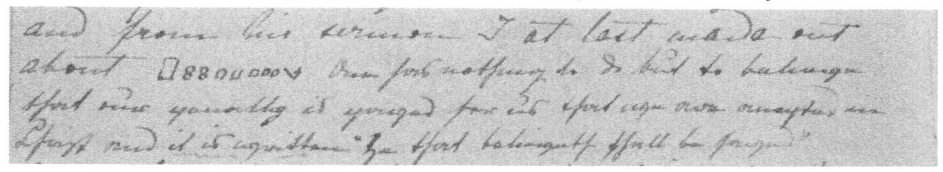

After afternoon service we all sat in the Beaumont grounds watching the sun on the mountains. Jack and I read hymns together, sitting inside a bush on the ground. We had music in the evening, and I got a letter from Lily with a private bit, asking for an opinion on a certain subject, so while my ideas were fresh in my head I wrote down my answer, as my ideas soon vanished. Jack and I are going solo to Luchon. I am at the height of happiness.

Pau, May 5, Monday

I practised, sang and put strings on my gown preparatory to going to the mountains, and read. Madame Fournier came. I rode with Jack on Mr Fitzgerald's grey horse, first down to the plain to watch the croquet going on. There were the two Powers and the 2 spooney boys and the three other girls, then on somewhere exploring among little brooks and green glades and odd little places until we got into the Biltère woods. Jack and Jin went to the PPC meeting and I went to sleep in the windows watching the stars and the lights and listening to Bess singing.

Pau, May 6, Tuesday

I went to finish my yesterday's lesson at Madame Fournier's. Galos came, and then we went off to be photographed [*by L Subercaze, 33, Rue Bayard (Haute Plante), Pau*]. Florence went with us, and we found there Mr Fitzgerald and Miss Tottenham who would keep peeping round corners at one. Cicell's and mine will be very good I think. I sang, then went to the Beaumont grounds and read Ruskin till it was time to dress to go to tea at the Martins. We walked there, Mama, Jin and I. The rest went to the Powers. There were the Hudsons, Hewills and somebody who I didn't know. We first had tea, then the PPC papers were read aloud. Talking went on during the rest of the evening. I was frightfully bored, having nobody young to talk to. Goodnight.

Pau, May 7, Wednesday

Galos came. Went to Church, etc. I went to bid the Packenhams goodbye as I shan't see them again, but I couldn't see them comfortably as they were just going out driving. I tried for Miss Hitchens, but there were people there so I did not go in. I rode with Jack all about the happy valley, exploring through green lanes and woods. O so jolly. The Corbets and Goffs came to tea, and again I was between Major Goff and Mr Corbet, but he did not stuff me so much as last time. We sang after tea and talked. We hope to meet them at Luchon. During our drawing lesson the Powers came, to whom I bid goodbye. I was greatly disgusted at Fanny refusing me her photograph when she promised it me before. I began to pack. Our photos came home, but mine does not please me much.

Journey, May 8, Thursday

Packed till 11, then set off on our travels with some neat carpet bags, etc. By dint of patience we got over the diligence journey to Tarbes where we landed, and a horrid place we found it. There were rats and vermin running about the floor of the eating room. We went to see the cathedral and dawdled about till the dilly was ready to go on to Bagnères. My pet pic [*peak*] went before us all the way, and I'm sure I saw the cabin on the top. At last we came to Bagnères which was only about as much in the mountains as Louvie and was not a bit like what I expected. We found the Holders here and got rooms next to them. We dined with them and there were also Capt. Story, Mr Harborde, Mr Philpotts. I hated the dinner, feeling horribly seedy and tired and longing to go to bed. After this disagreeable ceremony, I unpacked and went to bed.

Bagnères, May 9, Friday

Raining hard, pleasant for our first day. I began Ursula [*by Elizabeth Missing Sewell*] and played with the children and practised till luncheon, after which they made me sing and play a bit. It cleared soon, so Jack, Col. Holder and I went out. We did a little climbing, but I was longing to dispense with the Colonel, and have my stick, and all the others, and have a regular pull up a mountain, running all the way down instead of keeping to proper roads and talking or listening to twaddle, etc. Why do I dislike that man so much? I'm afraid of him, for I feel that I could never trust him. He would appear one thing and be another. Ugh! I altered my gown after I came in, and read all the evening. The Hepburns were expected, but a telegraphic message came to say that their coachman had driven them straight to Tarbes instead of coming here, so we shall not have them. I cannot say I'm sorry.

Bagnères, May 10, Saturday

I was nearly late for breakfast, having done some work instead of getting ready, at which people didn't seem very pleased. I wrote a bit to Cis, but could only do a little as we were going to the Cascade de Grip. Accordingly, off we went. The living drag came too, which we didn't want. In due time the village of Grip was reached, from whence we had to walk to the cascades. I had my mountain stick with me, which was very useful as it always was. The waterfall was very pretty, so I pulled out my book and sketched him. We then clambered up a little further and found another which I also sketched, then further still and Walter sketched this time. Blasting was going on near us, and it sounded so nice echoing among the rocks. We saw one big stone roll down. After this we ran down another way, but I had forgotten the way I used to jump down the mountains. The further I went the less tired I got; I suppose I'm getting into training. Such a state as my garments were in. Everybody held up their hands in astonishment as I got out of the carriage. We went out again after I was tidy and went all over the town, happy in not having the Drag with us for once. I've come to the conclusion that I am a beast! I read Ursula all the evening.

Bagnères, May 11, Sunday

Oh dear, why need it rain while we are in the mountains? We had English service in the French Church, which we were very glad of. After luncheon Jack and I slipped off, minus the Drag, and had a jolly walk among green paths and beech-trees and meadows and streams. So pretty as it was, and when we were tired we sat down for a bit to rest. It looked Sunday-like and fresh and was very pleasant. With Sunday discourses we cut shorter the way, and after our walk went to service again, but I was bored by continually finding the parson's eyes fixed upon me. Whether he thought I was not behaving properly, I don't know. Showers crept on at intervals all day, and it poured all the evening. They declared I was fast asleep in the evening, but I am sure I had only my eyes shut. I went to bed very early.

Bagnères, May 12, Monday

Rain again, which if it goes on will send us back to Pau in a hurry. Walter and I set off at 11 on a riding expedition, hoping that the rain would spare us, but not a bit of it. We had gone some way and walked up to a Calvaire [*Calvary*] which we had spied on top of a rock, when Mr Rain began to be felt. On we went for a bit, and at last made a tree into an umbrella and stood there till the drops came through. Then on we went again in the wind and rain, cantering where it was practicable, till a huge gust of wind cracked the stick of my umbrella and I had to go on without any. Canter, canter, canter, leaving the guide far behind, with all my hair down and greatly resembling Johnny Gilpin [*the subject of a comic ballad by William Cowper*] as a witch on a horse instead of a broomstick. We got so thoroughly soaked that we didn't mind getting wet any more, so it really was very jolly galloping all the way for more than ten miles I should think, without hardly stopping at all. It would have been a lovely road if it had been fair. Lots of men and women and dogs turned out to see us, and truly we must have been a fine sight. At last we got home, having had a very pleasant ride. I read Ruskin and Ursula and practised and played with the Babbies. My silence having been commented upon, I set to talking at dinner and was surprised at my success, but it's a horrid bore. I had a letter from Evelyn in which she wants me to stay with them. Won't it be jolly.

Journey, May 13, Tuesday

Raining again, which made us settle to go home at once, so I packed up my neat carpet bags again in readiness to start. The Holders went at 12, and we followed at 2 1/2. We were neither of us sorry, I believe, to part, which though sad to relate is true. We got alright to Tarbes and I took possession of the same room as before. The weather gave every appearance of having the intention to stop crying, so we demurred for some time whether we should go to Luchon or to Pau. We at last decided for the latter and got places accordingly. We had a fat Frenchman with us in the coupé who took up a great deal too much room and smelt of smoking odiously. We were such ages on the road that I thought they must be taking us to Cirès or Bayonne or some odd place, but finally the lights of Pau were seen and once more we passed through the well-known streets. The others were so astonished to see us back again, but we find all our friends have departed: Spencers, Packenhams, and Mr Somerset who has gone to Biarritz and is not coming back. I'm so sorry not to have said goodbye to him. We subscribed between us and sent him a present of 8 photographs which he valued greatly, and found out they were from Maison Dartigaux, though they were sent anonymously.* I'm so sorry they are all gone; it makes the place seem so melancholy and we have only 3 weeks more. Jin and I are to do the travelling through France, as Cis doesn't want to. We are to go to Luchon, as we did not see it before.

This may mean that the Grimstons were staying at Maison Dartigaux, or Hotel Dartigaux, on Rue Henri IV.

Pau, May 14, Wednesday

I did a commission for Helen and sent it her, and also wrote to Lily. In the afternoon we couldn't go out for the rain, so we played ball and impromptu duets once, and Catty and I began Quits [*a novel by Baroness Jemima von Tautphoeus*]. We read Quentin Durward [*Walter Scott*] in the evening.

Pau, May 15, Thursday

Practised and read in the morning. We 3 went to the singing meeting and came in late, much to our discomfiture. After it we went the Sunday walk and got such lots of flowers. The waterfall was too full to show much, the river was so swollen. Gussy, Fanny and Dickey came to tea in the evening. We all sang, me among others, and came out with a delightful skrake [*an Ulster word for screech*] instead of a high note. Fanny did give me her photo after all, at which I was pleased. Began cod. Ugh! [*What does this refer to, I wonder?*]

Pau, May 16, Friday

A new and important acquisition have I got today in the shape of portable property. Happening to remark that Walter's chain was dirty, I offered to clean it, so he said he had another thing which wanted cleaning. So I went with him to get it, upon which he pulled out a lovely Maltese filigree cross and said that as soon as I had cleaned him I might keep him. I did not refuse it. Mama and I went to the Bizanos wood, and while Mama sat down to read, I went and got forget-me-nots from the field below. They had passed their prime, but were still very beautiful. Then, after reading for some time, we went the round through the grounds and out at the other side. Alice and Constance came to tea and jabbered away all the evening, during which our eyelids felt the greatest inclination to shut. Blanche couldn't come, as she helps to nurse the scarletina child and is not allowed to see any of her friends for fear of infection. We have only 17 days more before leaving Pau.

Pau, May 17, Saturday
Finished Quits, which I like very much, but I don't intend to begin another yet, lest my taste for novels should grow too big. In the afternoon Jack, Bess and I went out riding. Gussy was to come with us, but when we went for her, her horse had not come, so we said we would go to visit the eagle and come back again, which we did, but meanwhile they had made a mess, imagining that we were not coming back, and sent Dickey to get a horse for himself as an escort to Gussy, so we waited for them both and then went somewhere about the coteaux. We were one time going up a very steep place when suddenly Bessie's, Gussie's and Walter's saddles all took to moving. This took some time to settle. We then proceeded and at last got onto a good road where Bess, I and Dickey had a gallop. Oh golly. From that time we went pretty fast, which was agreeable to my feelings, and as a finale at the bottom of the Montebello hill, Dickey proposed a race which I agreed to willingly and set off accordingly. Bess was soon deprived of breath and had to stop. Dickey and I were about even for some time but at last his horse gave in and I won it!!! I was so pleased. After that we had another gallop during which all my hair descended and my net was on the point of departure, so I had to get Dickey to hold my reins while I did up my wig again. My horse was a very wise one indeed, and pretty withal, and I hope to ride him again sometime.

Pau, May 18, Sunday
We heard that the grey pony departed this life, at which Mama was grieved. Poor thing, I'm sorry it is done for. The extra child was stuck in our pew again today and was squashed accordingly. Sadly

Lifford, the youngest Hewitt, and Bona Spencer came to tea after church and stayed too long, as the others had settled to go with the Powers. However, they managed to slip out and Jack and I followed afterwards. The rendezvous was the Basterreches garden, and we were bored at finding Captain Bury snugly ensconced beside Gussy. Poor Bess was soon after left as gooseberry. We had gone to another place, and Cis and Fanny departed together. We settled in the evening that no more gooseberries should be acted, but from henceforth we should leave them to their own devices.

Pau, May 19, Monday

Madame Fournier came. I wrote to Eve, began Cleve Hall [*by Elizabeth Missing Sewell*] and Recreations, etc. In the afternoon, Walter and I went a huge long walk. We set off by the Sunday walk and crossed the river at the little waterfall; we got over a laddery bridge which was thrown across the stones, and I felt as if I was going at telegraph pace to the left, and the water standing still, so I had to keep my eyes on the opposite bank lest I should topple over. We followed the river all along among ferns and shady trees and all sorts of nice things, till we saw a dear little bridge peeping out the trees, which I sketched, and Walter told me what to do. Then we followed our noses, which led into the Bizanos wood far on. We explored a good deal and then came back through the wood, crossed the road and came home by the nightingales wood. So there's a good walk for any young woman methinks. Eh?!! In the evening Mama, Bess, and Cis went to tea at the Liffords, and we 3 ensconced ourselves in a row on the sofa with our feet on chairs and read. So snug!

Pau, May 20, Tuesday

Such a lazy day as I have spent today. I finished my letter to Evelyn and then read Cleve Hall. Jin and I went shopping and soon came in again as it was drizzle. Dear me, I forgot the chief event of the day: the wedding! We went to the chapel near the

Duke's house, with Fanny, a little before 10. In due time the organ began a puffing tune and in came the party. The bridegroom turned out to be not the little boy we thought, but another man with a truly ugly French face. The bride looked very serene and smiling, and was attired in a white silk dress with deep flounces of lace and furbelows of tulle, and a long tulle veil on top of a wreath of orange flowers and clematis. She looked very yellow with so much white about her. Such a mockery as it all seemed. The people certainly knelt down, but instead of saying their prayers they looked about them all the time and talked to their friends. I'm thankful I was not born a Romanist.

Pau, May 21, Wednesday

Practised, sang and read Recreations and Cleve Hall. In the afternoon I went with Walter to the Castle terrace to sketch the Thurlows house. I ensconced myself on the wall among some bushes where I should not be much seen, and sketched. Walter had to go out riding with Cis and the Spencers at 5, and I had not finished my drawing, so he left me there for the chance of picking up Mama and Maude, which however I did not do, but came home alone at which I felt proud of being so brave. The Alexanders came for some time, but I did not trouble myself much to talk to them as the others were there too. How passing is favour in people's eyes! But one day ago I was nearly first with somebody. Now it is very different, and that for <u>one</u> word!!

Pau, May 22, Thursday

Madame Fournier came, and while she was still here the Powers came, and Gussy would stand over me, which put the old woman into such an excited state of wanting me to play well, that of course it had the contrary effect. In the afternoon we 3 went to the meeting which is to be the last one. Then Jack, Jin, Puss and I went for a walk to the nightingale wood. I said adieu to my promontory, dear old place. The river was rushing past as of yore, yet how different is the person who was so happy there last year, and the creature of this year, not that I mean the 1st was the happiest. Then we sat for a bit on some planks and listened to the music of the woods, and admired the long poplars always striving upward. Then on we went through thick and thin to the bank of the river, which looked so calm and placid with all the trees reflected in it like a very happy person reflecting their peace around and making others happy too. Onward yet through bushes and by banks of crimson clover and convolvulus and at last up through the Beaumont grounds home. When I came in, Bess told me that I had forgotten the unfortunate Ina with whom I was to have walked. I feel very repentant, but glad I had this walk.

Pau, May 23, Friday

Read "Recreations", practised and sang and finished Cleve Hall. Ronald is a beautiful character, so noble. In the afternoon we went out riding, a party of ten composed of Sir John, Gussy, Fanny, Walter, Maude, me, Mr Unwin, Mrs Fraser, sister to the Grogan, Capt. Bury and Mrs Blackeny, a snob of snobs, the snobbest. I had the grey horse and was accordingly 100 yards in front of the others all the time. We went to Pieta by some odd road which joined the proper one, and didn't get home till very late. The sunset was beauteous - a round red ball sinking into a golden bed. Rich!! I had a nice talk with Sir John who was with me most of the time, a most comfortable talk I may say.

Pau, May 24, Saturday

Tried to finish my sketch of the Thurlows house, but made a mess thereof. I went out with Ina and Amelia to the nightingale wood, and we sat for a long time on my promontory discussing books and many subjects. At last we were chased away by a man fishing, so we dawdled about till it was time to take Amelia home. We deposited her safe, then Ina and I went to the Bastarreches garden and sat in the laurel passage. I

attacked her then and found she was right, but rather weedy.
Oh dear, I wish I could learn to speak, but I was recompensed
afterwards by... [*Rest of the sentence indecipherable (see below).*]

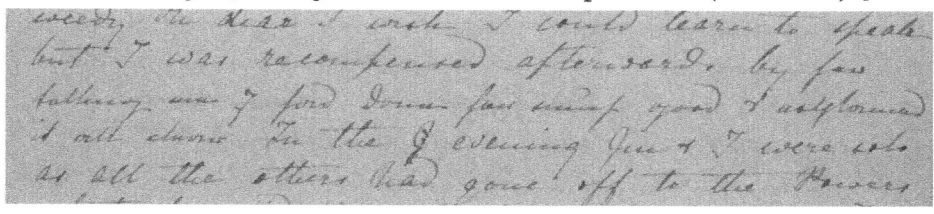

In the evening, Jin and I were solo as all the others had gone off
to the Powers. What they did there I do not know yet. I played all
the reveries I possessed and then sang, after which I conversed
with my friends portraits, an unfailing source of pleasure to
me. From the others account of the Powers, they seem to have
had great fun and I shouldn't have minded being there myself.

Pau, May 25, Sunday

Our all but last Sunday, and not a pretty one. 2 of us moved
out into a different pew during each of the services, as
there were many vacant. A sermon was preached for
the factory people. We were so disappointed at the HC
not being given out. We hoped to have had it once more
here, but Whitsunday comes next, so that's why.

Pau, May 26, Monday

Drizzle and spit all day. I practised, sang and read. In the afternoon
we went shopping. I got some pen-holders for each of my boys.
Then I went and sketched the Thurlows house from the Basses
Plantes, which sketch looks more promising than the other:
then we 4 trudged up to the cemetery, pulling each other up the
big hill, and roamed about for a bit till a thought of tea called us
home again, after which we attired ourselves in beauteous array
for our wee party, which there enumerate Mr and Mrs Hudson,
Weekeses, Powers, Kate, Capt Bury, Mr Unwin, Little Kane, Mr

Philpott and Spencers. I think that's all. Of course I was sent as a pretender to the music. Gussy sang and Mr Unwin whistled, and duets and glees came in between-whiles. I talked principally to Kate, Bona and Dickey and I think everybody enjoyed themselves.

Pau, May 27, Tuesday

I drew, practised, etc, all the morning and rode in the afternoon. There was a party of 10 riding: Sir John, Gussy, Capt. Bury, Mr Blackney, Kate, Mrs Fraser, Jack, Bess, Cis and me. We went all over the coteaux somewhere. Coming home, 3 of us had such a jolly gallop. Of course I was one, and it was about the best part of the ride, for people w'd canter so slow and my horse would go fast, so I was always ahead, consequently laughed at. We came into the town in a line, looking very imposing, and I was pretty well done up after it.

Pau, May 28, Wednesday

A lazy morning did I spend, namely reading my last year's journal. In the afternoon I went to the Beaumont grounds, maybe for the last time, as we have settled to go away on Saturday. Fancy my having only 2 days more!! Mama, Jin and I then went to tea at the Liffords, where there appeared Mrs Taylor and Amelia and the Philpotts. We didn't stay long as we heard more people were coming, but went to call on the Gilbert Smiths who we found at home, but I had nobody to talk to and was glad to get away at last. Walter told us in the evening that all the brothers had conspired to get Mama a pair of horses. Won't it be nice, we do feel so proud, for then we shall be as grand as our neighbours.

Pau, May 28, Thursday

Went to Church for the last time here, so bid goodbye to the old place. After church we went to Miss Hay's and did the same there. Margaret presented me with her photograph, without my asking for it even, and the old one walked to the stairs with my hand fast in hers. In the afternoon we intended to go to Madame Gillemains for a species of picnic with the Weekeses and Ina Spencer who had come to see me. Bess, Maude and I rode with Walter and Sir John and the others were in the carriage. But that horrid rain caught us half way and sent us riders home again in a hurry. I had Mrs Cliffe's old horse and I amused myself by repeating bits of 'Johnny Gilpin' as I cantered along in time to the jog. Jack went on to tell the others we were not coming, so he got all our nice strawberries which we were to have had.

Pau, May 30, Friday

Och noue, och noue, sure and is it the last time that the craitur'll be able to git Pau to disturb the line of white paper at the top of each day? Sure an' it is, yur Honour and hard work she'll find it to keep the scrivnah from a writin' of it still (the pen I mean) for yr Honour I always find that my pig'll run to the same trough he's accustomed to. What rubbish! I must try and be sensible. I stayed in all day to pack and was well tired after it all. My poor little domicile does look so bare without its picture, sentence and rosary, and to think that I shall never see it more. Most of the others went to the Countess Kallings in the evening, where they were bored greatly.

Journey, May 31, Saturday

For the last time have I had to tumble out of my dear little bed. The last touches are put to my packing, the last look at my room, and we depart for the 'dilly', laden with a big bouquet from the concierge, and umbrellas. Now we are off through the well-known streets down which we gaze lovingly, looking out for familiar faces, none of which we see except Dr Ottley. By degrees we got sleepy and our thoughts wander to many incidents which have happened, mixed with interesting conversations and jokes written down in one's memory. Finally we arrive at Tarbes, and avoiding the Rat Hotel go to another, a far better one, where we eat and then sally forth to the Cathedral. We were soon again in the 'dilly', jogging towards Bagnères in a pelt. Our old rooms at the Hotel de Paris receive us and we are snug once more. Jin and I share my room, Jack has Col. Holder's and our weary bodies soon were resting in bed.

Bagnères. June 1, Sunday

We heard that there would be the HC, so Jin and I settled to stay, which we did and it was very nice. I did like going to the little Church again, and to my old place in it so much. We couldn't go out at all, it was pouring, so we had to amuse ourselves as best we could. Jack and Jin had a long disputation about bands on Sunday, which bored me, so I departed. The evening was spent most unprofitably, namely Walter teazing me. He would stick his fingers in my mouth and punch me, etc, and pull off my net till I got to a pitch of untidiness, when I subsided for the night.

Bagnères, June 2, Monday

Worked and drew in the morning. We also went all over the shady walks where Jack and I went on the Sunday we were here before. We were to have driven in the afternoon, but the rain put his finger in the pie and prevented till too late, so instead we went up to the flagstaff on top of the mountain seen from our windows, and hard work we found it, as we had not our sticks. We hopped down again pretty quick and came home in a nice state of wet and dirt, but glad we had done it. The view was very pretty from the top and we could trace nearly all our wild-goose ride. The teazing process went on. In the evening I began writing a story, but failed from stupidity.

Bagnères to Luchon, June 3, Tuesday

We set off at 7 1/2 and went by the plain, amusing ourselves solving the problem of how the corn could be in rows wherever one looked. We sketched the old castle at Mauveoisin from the carriage, and the rest of the way my gloves ran a good chance of being worn out from coming in contact with a warm sort of substance called hand. We stopped at 2 different places on the way, the first we explored, the 2nd we kept quiet and fed upon sour bread, rancid butter and unripe cherries. Off we set again, our road leading us by such splendid marble rocks and cascades and a boiling torrent and all the cottages were marble halls. Such loveliness as we passed and at last drove up an avenue and landed in the Hotel d'Angleterre which was frightfully dear, but jolly rooms where we were not long in going to bed. We went and inquired the prices at the hotels and settled to go to the Bains where the Hepburns are. As we passed the windows we saw the whole family at dinner, so had to give a skip past lest they should spy us. O, I'm so sleepy.

Luchon, June 4, Wednesday

Packed up our goods and sent them off to the Hotel des Bains, and after conferring with the guide we settled to go to Antieade [?] and to Antieade we went with four nags. Jin nearly came to grief in her first canter, but stuck on ever after. There were such huge mountains close to us with glaciers on them, and high wooded ones as pedestals; my horse grew sleepy on the way up, so sat down comfortably and prepared for a roll, which, poor thing, it was not allowed to have after all. In time the top was gained and we looked all round. The Maladetta poked his hoary head above all the rest, and our guide showed us the way we should have to go if we went there, all through the snow. Next we had to feed, so we got a lot of snow and brandy, our mountain beverage, and were enjoying our victuals when another small party came tumbling up. They were English, so we invited them to partake of our fare, but they didn't seem to like being spoken to, so we adjourned to a neighbouring knoll and there sat to bake and watch the clouds rising from earth to heaven. We got a lot of flowers, as it was like a garden with all the daphne and gentian and narcissi, but my flowers managed to jump out of my pocket coming home, so I have not many left. We had dinner with the Hepburns, at which nobody took much pains to talk, so pauses ensued which were rather uncomfortable. I have a dear little room to myself here, which is pleasant. Goodnight.

Luchon, June 5, Thursday
Jin was done up with yesterday, so Walter and I went off alone to the Lac d'Oô. The road there was lovely, and I sketched one piece. We were not long getting to the lake, which I thought well worth going to. I did a sketch of a waterfall just before one comes to it. But rainy clouds were seen coming nearer, and soon we were obliged to take refuge in a cabin where the horses were put up. Here we found a ladder, so clambered up to a loft above, and made a boy break open a nailed-up window to let a little light on the scene. The guide warned us that animals inhabited the loft, but we paid no heed to him and spread out our luncheon on an old bench in front of us and demolished our eatables. The rain kindly ran away for a bit, so we went out and I scrambled down by the lake and gathered flowers and watched the shadows and the fishes, while Walter followed a path leading to the second lake. While I was amusing myself standing on a stone in the lake, a low sort of muttering growl was heard, which grew louder and louder by degrees, till it turned into thunder pealing overhead, which echoed so grandly among the mountains. It was so nice, but now it began to pour so I had to rush into the stable again. Walter soon after returned, and as there seemed no prospect of its clearing, we set out again for home, from time to time waiting under a tree or a rock till the rain grew less heavy. As soon as the road got tolerable, we went a pace and hardly stopped till we got home well drenched but very glad we had done it. I got a letter from Lily.

Luchon, June 6, Friday
This time the Hepburns came with us and we went up a mountain called Super Bagnères all through a pine forest. We ate on the

top and hunted butterflys and flowers. We came home another way having to go down a very steep heathy place where we got so tired of hopping and sliding and tumbling. The rain caught us again, so we didn't go up the Vallée du Lis as we intended, but only to the entrance and then home. I talked a good deal to Mary and liked her much, as also Janey but t'other don't suit me exactly. I wrote to Cis in the evening to amuse myself.

Luchon, June 7, Saturday

Off at 8 to do the Pic de Boccanière [*probably Pic de Bacanere on the Spanish border*] Jin's love of cantering increasing rapidly. It was baking and a long way to go, but finally we got to the top, being still in France, but having clambered down the bank we were told we were in Spain. We ate in France, and then Jack and I went on to do a Pic a little further off, from whence a huge extent of plain could be seen. However, I stuck half way, my legs forsaking me, and waited while Walter went on. We had to hop a long way during which I nearly subsided coming down again, and we were terribly tired when we got home, besides our faces being burnt crimson. We are looking forward to Sunday so much. What a blessing it will be to rest, only we will not have any Church to go to.

Luchon, June 8, Sunday

A hash between Jack and me about his being so fond of me. Oh, it is so horrid.

A parson did turn up, so we had service after all in the large hall, so that was nice. We afterwards went to the gardens with Miss Weekes, and sat there till a thunder storm came and drove us in to luncheon. I wrote up my journal in the afternoon, as I had left it for 2 or 3 days. We have come to the conclusion that Jin and I are not up to the Maladetta, as we feel the worse for wear after all our expeditions, and Walter thinks so too, so that's settled. We are getting to like the Hepburns immensely. How different from what we thought before. We had great fun sitting outside the hall door after dinner, and stayed there till very late talking.

Luchon, June 9, Monday

Raining, which looks melancholy. Nevertheless, it clearing in the afternoon we went off to the Vallée de Lys to see all the cascades, in a carriage with Sir Thomas and Mary. Jin got out to sketch on the way, leaving Mary and me solo, on which the hitherto silent Mary set to and talked like two, and a very pleasant bit of time we had. We drove nearly to the end of the valley, and then walked to the cascades, the paths leading to them being occupied by little torrents through which we had to pass as best we could. There were some beautiful falls, one of which we sketched, and then came down again in a nice soaked state, having been in a weeping cloud all the time, added to the small torrents that were running wherever we had to go, filling our boots with water and making our petticoats drip like umbrellas. We walked on and got lots of lovely white lilies with which the valley was filled, and were picked up by the carriage and carried home again. In the evening the Hepburns asked us to come up to them, so we did and enjoyed it much. Miss Hepburn played very well indeed and I sang 2 things, and the rest of the time we talked and stood on the balcony watching the stars.

Luchon, June 10, Tuesday

Baking and sunny once more, so Jack knocked us up to go to the Port de Venasque [*a mountain pass*] as a crowning expedition. We had a carriage as far as the Hospice [*de France*] and there mounted our little nags for the last time. We went up zigzag a long way, being nearly blown down every now and then, till we got to a large patch of snow where we had to dismount and walk the rest of the way up. Just as we were going to cross the snow, a Spaniard who was coming the other way over it slipped and went down about 100 yards. It was very exciting watching him slip faster and faster till at last he stopped on a rock at the bottom and grinned up at us. We had to cross 3 large patches of snow, and after a good deal of panting and puffing arrived at the top, and passing through the Port sat down on a rock in Spain just opposite the Maladetta. Jack was not half satisfied with the climb so he and the guide went on to the Sauvegarde, a Pic higher up, where he stuck down his name in a book which lives on the top. Jin and I meanwhile waited and waited, wondering when their Majesties would turn up again, and eating from time to time. At last they came, much to our relief, and after eating and sketching the Port we hobbled down again in double quick time, paid a last farewell to our horses and drove into Luchon in grand style. On our way the guide took us to the Parisienne cascade, which was very pretty indeed. We were quick over dinner and then packed up our goods as we were going away at 9 1/2 that evening. I was bold enough to ask Mary Hepburn for her photograph, which she gave willingly and also brought me Jane's, which Jin clutched, but I got one too. It was soon time for the farewells, of which there were many to do. Then we jumped into the carriage and away we went, leaving quite a crowd watching our departure, and turning our backs on the mountains forever. I had forgotten to leave my old boots behind, so tossed them into a cart as we passed it, and I hope they will be duly appreciated. We grew very sleepy indeed, and it was 2 o'clock when we got to Labarthe where we were to sleep. On our arrival we were told that the hotel was pretty much filled, but after considering for a bit they said we c'd perhaps be stowed in somewhere. So Jin and I were put in a room which looked as if a broom had not the honour of its acquaintance, and as if it was the chickens' favourite promenade, with rat holes in the floor and several capital hiding places for robbers. Nevertheless, our slumbers were not the less sound, though we were not sorry to depart next morning.

ARTHUR C. VENTRESS

Journey, June 11, Wednesday

We went on early to Tarbes, where we met the Unwins who came into our carriage, and we had them as far as Mont de Marsan. We went to Bayonne, and from thence by omnibus to Biarritz with some absurd English people who amused us immensely by the way they went on. It was late when we got to Biarritz, so we went to the Hotel for the night. The sea did look so lovely by moonlight, dashing up against the black rocks. I could hardly go away from the window it was so lovely. Our room was rather a contrast to last night's and feels quite like a palace in comparison.

Biarritz, June 12, Thursday

Before breakfast we sallied forth to find the others, but hearing that they wouldn't appear for a long time yet we went to the rocks and sat for a bit until our lazy family came downstairs, when we had a happy meeting. Bess and I went again to the rocks, and we gave our several accounts of our grand doings to each other. It is pleasant having a bit of a rest here, which I do want very badly. We read novels, and sit out all day, a lazy life enough, but very comfortable. We also had a grand singing match at the hotel, where I shouted to my heart's content.

Biarritz, June 13, Friday

Took it easy all day, sketching the rocks and reading. I began 'John Halifax' [*John Halifax, Gentleman by Dinah Craik, 1856*] and cannot help reading it till I'm stupid. I took a walk all by myself along the shore and all over and sketched from a pinnacle of rock the Spanish mountains. Here Jack found me and came home with me. He, Jin and Bess are going to Tours tomorrow. I'm too glad of quiet to wish to leave it yet. Cis and I squealed our duet over at the hotel for a long time.

Biarritz, June 14, Saturday

The others set off on their travels. Our day was passed as usual, sketching, reading and walking. I replenished my remembrance book and packed some of my box. The Davides have taken part of our house, so we are continually overlooked, which is a bore. We have only 13 days before getting home. How funny it seems.

Biarritz, June 15, Sunday

Went to Mr Crow's dear little church in the morning, and he gave us a capital sermon, though not quite so good as I expected. We were so sleepy all day. After dinner I went to sleep and felt refreshed after it. I then sallied forth to go and bid the rocks goodbye, but there were too many people for me to go by myself. I found Maude and Cis prowling about near the boats, getting maidenhair, so I joined them, and afterwards went with Maudey to the rocks, but were chased by some Frenchmen all the way, so not approving of their vicinity we soon came away again. Such work as we had to shut our boxes. Mine resisted all our efforts, so had to be left for stronger claws. My affection for Biarritz has not had time to thrive yet, so I'm not much grieved at leaving, especially with such a bright star as home in the distance. So farewell Biarritz, my dear.

Journey, June 16, Monday

Once more up and away, rattling over the stones in an omnibus for Bayonne, where after much jolting we arrived in peace. We were put into a "Dames" carriage [*this must be a railway carriage, as the distance from Bayonne to Paris is around 400 miles*] and had the usual plague on such occasions, a fretful baby besides being 8 inside. This went on as far as Bordeaux, where we had to stop for 2 hours, so took care to go the other way from the baby getting in again. We filled up as much space as possible in our carriage, and I put up my feet and pretended to be a great invalid, so as to keep people out. Also Mama stood at the window looking very sour. This dodge completely succeeded and though many people opened the door, they none of them dared come in, so we were comfortable all the way to Paris and made beds out of cloaks and slept. We got to Paris about 5 1/2, so as soon as we were settled in a hotel and had breakfast, we each had a bath and went to bed, except me as I didn't think I needed any more slumber, so wrote my journal instead.

Paris, June 17, Tuesday

Some of us went to see the Madeleine in the morning, as it is close to our house. It was a very pretty place, but a pity that it should have been Catholic. An old man at the entrance would keep shaking a brush [*holy water brush?*] at us full of incense or something of the sort and looked so horrified when we didn't take it. After the Madeleine we went to shop, and on our way we spied Mr Fitzgerald, so attacked him, and he told us that Mrs Fitz was very near and would like to see us, so off we went and sat with her for a bit. After that we went shopping again and bought some dear little parasols. We couldn't help thinking that every dandified looking man that we met must be a pickpocket, so looked well after our purses and lockets. Our legs began now to complain, so back we came and found the others come, having been to Orleans, Tours, Blois, etc, etc and seen no end of cathedrals and things. In the evening we heard there was to be a concert in the Tuileries Gardens, so out we trudged once more but found no concert at all. Walking along we met Miss Tottenham and her brother, so talked to them and then sat down in a lump under an orange-tree till it was time for the gardens to be closed, when we went to the Place de la Concorde and pictured to ourselves the guillotine and the women knitting and counting the heads as they fell. Not having had enough yet, we went out driving in two cabs to see all the lighted-up shops and the lights in the river. I, however, was so sleepy that I could hardly open my eyes enough to blink, so didn't much enjoy this part of the entertainment.

Paris, June 18, Wednesday

After breakfast we went off to Notre Dame, and were greatly disappointed in the outer part where the services were done, it being all gaudily painted, but no pretty carving, but when we got to the inner part we were delighted. It was all in confusion with workmen, so didn't show to the best advantage, but there were such exquisite painted windows and carvings and was quite beautiful. While we were there we heard the organ going on in the outer part, so went and listened to it. They were doing a mass for somebody's soul, and the chanting was so beautiful, all in the minor, done by the rolling organ and the priests alone. Then some boys joined in with treble voices. O so pretty. As soon as the music stopped, the others went off to the Fitzgeralds, and Jack, Maude, Cis and me to see the Emperor's Chapel. We ought to have got leave to go in from the Minister of State, but we made out a pleading story of not having time to get leave before going away, so they let us in and we were delighted with it. Nearly all the walls were painted glass windows. There was only a tiny bit of wall between each window, and the painted glass gave such a beautiful soft light all round, just the sort of place one should like to do one's devotions in. The Chapel was built by St. Louis, and they showed us the stall which he always used, with one opposite for his mother. Also a closet where Louis XI used to go to hear mass, with a little window to hear it through as he was always afraid of being murdered if he was with other people. From that we passed into the Palais de Justice through the same door as Victoria had gone through when she was last in Paris, and we saw all the lawyers in their gowns with huge books of parchment under their arms. It was now time for luncheon, so back we came and after that all went off to the Louvre as it was raining and we couldn't do anything else. We went through dozens of rooms, but were terribly disappointed with the pictures. They were not half as beautiful as we expected, though some were very good. The others went off to the Palais Royale afterwards, but I was too tired, so stayed in.

ARTHUR C. VENTRESS

Paris, June 19, Thursday

We set off early to do Versailles. After about 1/2 an hour of train, we got out and were jolted off to a hotel where we feasted and then went on to the palace, the little Trianon, where Marie Antoinette used to retire to when she was tired of the cares of state, and she used to have her little farm to look after. We didn't go over the house, but went all over the grounds which were delicious, so green and shady and with such lots of dear little curling paths all over and a pretty little lake with trees hanging into it. After we had done this we got into our vehicles again and went to see the Emperor's carriages, at which Cis went into ecstasies, such grand things as they were all gilt with flowers and cherubs painted on them. We touched Marie Antoinette's sedan chair and Charles VIth's carriage in spite of numerous placards put up to forbid us. After this we went all over the big Trianon and saw the Empress Josephine's bedroom with its gilt bed and balusters before it, and the grand drawing-rooms and council room of which all the walls nearly were mirrors and everything grand. We then went to a hotel to eat in preparation for the fatigue of going over the palace. After we had well supported ourselves we set out again for the Palais, and were first ushered up a tremendously grand staircase to a long gallery full of statues of the French kings and queens and grand people. From that into long suites of rooms crammed with huge pictures of battles, far superior to anything in the Louvre. Really, they made one quite long to be a soldier and fight. It made us quite excited. We were so amused, and got cross at seeing how the English were all represented as being killed or running away in the battles of Alma and Inkermann, and the French pressing onward towards the enemy. Mama hated these pictures, for there were always dreadfully wounded people in the foreground. I didn't mind them myself at all, I suppose, being of a bloodthirsty nature. We hadn't time to enjoy these things half enough, but had to rush through the last room as we wanted to see the gardens a bit, so down we went, and hearing a band going on somewhere we went towards it and sat down under some bushes to listen to it. Jack afterwards found a much nicer place, so we all went there and revelled in the music. It was the most exquisite band I have ever heard, and I should have liked to listen to it forever, but time flies apace and we had soon to depart to catch the train, having enjoyed today the most of any. It was delicious. When we arrived at the Paris Station we saw a suspicious-looking man get out of the train and walk away arm in arm with a worse-looking man still, so we watched them, feeling certain that they were two pickpockets. They whispered together for some time and then sidled up close to Mama's pocket side. At this Cis ran up to warn Mama, on which the pickpockets, with a lowering glance at us, moved away into the crowd, keeping their eye on us, however, till we could see them no more. We were so proud of having seen two real pickpockets among the Paris sights. We packed all the evening. So ended Versailles.

Journey, June 20, Friday

Left Paris, for many a year I hope, at 9. The train was very full, so Jack and I were alone in one carriage with some other people, and the others were parcelled out elsewhere. Our companions were all absurd: a man just like Mr Arden, and his wife, a nervous old hag who screamed at the slightest noise. Jack, in getting down the shawls, let one tumble on her feet, on which she screamed. "I hope I didn't hurt you," said Jack. "No," said she, in a hurt and plaintive tone, "but you frightened me." Then there were two governesses, one of which put her veil so as to hide herself from Jack who was beside her, and I'm sure she was no beauty, so I sketched her and the nervous old dame. The latter found me out so covered her face with her handkerchief, but I had already got it well in my head and went on nevertheless. When we got to Dieppe, we met the Hendersons who were just seeing their governess off to England. We were so enchanted at the sailors on the steamer, being English.

And now the steamer is unmoored and we leave France without a tear, from henceforth turning our backs to it. On the vessel, as we well know, Jin is regardless of appearances, so she rolled herself up in a large grey railway rug, doffed her bonnet, bundled her head up in Bessie's capulet and laid down in the middle of the deck, thus bearing a striking resemblance to a pig in a sack rolling about on a railway platform, as one sometimes sees. We others sat up tidily in a row, cracking jokes at the expense of the other passengers. There was a German just opposite us who from time to time gave Bess and me such approving smiles, we being about the best sailors there were. Poor Mama and Jin gave themselves up very soon to the tender mercies of the sea, but Jack had taught us how to fight against it, i.e. never to let the sea leave us behind, but to go with it partout. This saved us till just at the last when Jin set an example which was followed by nearly all the passengers, and alas, me among them!! But now the white cliffs of Newhaven appear in sight and we are once again on English ground. We were packed directly into the train for London and arrived there in peace. Oh, how nice it was to hear nothing but English! Three cabs bore us and our luggage to our lodgings, the owner of which was a real Yorkshire woman, accent and all. We feasted with delight on English bread and butter and then departed to bed, content and happy as could be.

London, June 21, Saturday
We slumbered long and sound and had breakfast at a fashionable hour, after which the others went off to see Floss, and Jin and I to Nina, but she was just gone out. I got a dear little new bonnet as Floss condemned our old ones. During dinner Aunt Mary and Addy turned up. They told us that Addie was going to be married to a Capt. Shouldham. We invited them to tea, to which they came. Jack and Cis went off to see the Stuart Trenches and brought home Uncle Hen with them. Mama also came, so we had a grand reception and much chatteration went on.

London, June 22, Sunday

Nobody could decide which Church to go to, but at last Jack, Jin, Cis and I went to a dear little Church, I forget its name, and by bribing the pew opener got very good seats in the gallery. There was such an exquisite anthem in which a tenor voice sung solo, and lovely it was. The Archbishop of York preached, but only a very stupid sermon, whereupon we were greatly disappointed. Jack, Jin and I went to luncheon at the Sandersons, where I was in a great fright and very glad to go away, though glad to have seen Frank. In the afternoon we went to the South Audley Street Church [*probably the Grosvenor Chapel*] which I didn't like a bit. Happening to raise my eyes to the Gallery, I saw a familiar face at which my heart set a wiggling waggling at a great rate, namely the Mountgarret family with Fanny and Clare. How I was longing to get at her to be sure, but when we got out I could see no traces of her anywhere, though I searched all about for her dear little face. Disconsolate, I went towards home when Jack proposed a turn in Rotten Row. This was not exactly a Sunday amusement, but for once in a way we agreed there would be no harm in it. So thither we bent our steps and looked out for all the pretty girls. Sitting at a corner we descried Gussie, Fanny, Dickey and Mr Somerset, so went and discoursed with them. I was glad to see Mr Somerset again as I had never said goodbye to him. On we proceeded and met Mr Rudd and Col. Hume and last of all, turning my eyes to the right, I saw Fanny Butler running at me full tilt. In my delight I nearly leapt over a chair, and as it was I tore a lot of trimming off my frock. How we chattered and laughed and talked. She was just as much delighted to see me as I was to see her, a most satisfactory little being, she had grown so pretty and nice-looking and we parted again with many hopes of meeting somewhere. We got home dreadfully late for dinner. After it, Mama, Jin, Maude and I went to Westminster Abbey and found the Dean just going into Church,* so we sent a man to get us seats. My seat was beside a chorister, and under one of the reading desks, so I felt very like a clerk. In the hymn, the chorister gave me his book. I wondered why the tune was quite different and I discovered that he had given me the part which he sang. The Dean only did a little of the service. I felt very frightened, for I was also within a yard of him and Mrs Dean. We met Uncle Stuart and Anna coming out of the Abbey, so talked a piece to them, and Uncle Stuart came home with us and stayed all the evening. I do like him so much. He promised to take some of us into the slums of London, at which we were delighted and had great fun with him. I thought Anna so pretty, with such a sweet expression, though rather sad-looking. I should not have called her lovely.

The dean was Richard Chenevix Trench (1807-86), writer and poet. He may have been related to Octavia's mother, also a Trench, though she does not mention it. Richard Trench instituted Sunday evening services in the abbey's nave.

London, June 23, Monday

The day of the Handel Festival "The Messiah". Jin, Mama and I set out earlier than the others, they having to get some bonnets. The train was crammed, so we were all separated, which at a London station was not pleasant. However, we joined again at the Crystal Palace, and after hunting for a long time found our places and ensconced ourselves in them. The seats were filled by degrees, while a low muttering of instruments tuning went on. There were 4000 performers. As the clock struck they began "God Save the Queen" and everybody had to stand, which I did not feel inclined to do. Such a grand chorus as it made. They then began the oratorio, which made one creep "all of a thrimble" it was too beautiful. There were three people who sang solos: Miss Dolby [*Charlotte Dolby, contralto, 1821-85*], Sims Reeves [*John Sims Reeves, tenor, 1821-1900*] and Mlle Titiens [*Therese Carolina Tietjens, soprano, 1831-77*]. The latter's voice was something exquisite. A soprano, she sang "He shall feed his flock", etc, and I thought it the best of all. Between the 1st and 2nd part, George and Lily Colley came up to us and talked for a bit. Mama asked them to tea, which they accepted. We saw no other people that we knew, and soon the music began again. We came home directly after it was over, feeling decidedly better for it. George and Lily turned up soon, and we had a jolly evening. I felt very jealous, for Lily didn't seem to care for me at all. We thought George very handsome and liked him very much.

London, June 24, Tuesday

After breakfast Mama, Jin and I went to the exhibition [*South Kensington*]. We went all over the French court, up the nave, then to the pictures which were beautiful, then all over the galleries. Saw some lovely models in cork of cathedrals and after all this I was regularly done so we came home. I am so tired of looking at things that I don't care to go again. We found Mrs and Mary Stewart in the drawing-room when we got home. Cis had Gertie up in her room. Maude and I behaved terribly, for we were in fits at Mrs Stewart all the time, poor old thing. A lot of us went to the Pantheon* in the afternoon, that place of ruin, and didn't my money go quick? In the evening the Marins and Uncle Hen appeared to tea. I was frightfully tired and truly glad to go to bed. How nice and quiet home will be.

The Pantheon was a place of public entertainment on the south side of Oxford Street, designed by James Wyatt and opened in 1772.

London, June 25, Wednesday

Fan came in the morning, also ---- Vernon and Addie. Jack, Jin, Bess and I went to a review at Woolwich, where we met Marin. We got to a capital place, close to the Duke of Cambridge who did the reviewing. The soldiers first walked past, then trotted, then cantered, they looking so jolly. Then they acted a siege or something of the sort, and the guns went firing so hugely loud that one's ears felt the worse for wear. At the guns, the horses of the spectators set to capering and jumping about so nicely that it was pleasant to watch them. The review didn't last very long, but it was rather headachy work. Nobody came to tea tonight, so we took to bed. Fan had Jack's room, we having prevented her going home as she intended.

London, June 26, Thursday

Nina came to breakfast. She was just the same as ever, and looking so nice with her little short hair. Jack liked her very much. We spent a nice lazy morning talking to her, and then took her home again and looked at her pictures, such grand ones as they were, among them the blue Madonna at Grimston and so beautifully painted. We saw her brother George also, and then went with her to see her sister, such a duck as she was. I did like her so much and was longing to kiss her. After this, Fan and most of us went to the Pantheon and I made Cis buy lots of things and wouldn't buy anything myself. Will and Annie came in the evening, our first sight of Annie.

Then this cryptic sentence follows, which may contain uncomplementary verdicts on Annie and Bill.

Bill was grown huge in breadth.

Journey Home, June 27, Friday

Set off in 3 cabs again, one of which contained Jack and me, and were soon on our way northwards again. Saw our sweet Howden tower [*Howden Minster*] and got out at dirty old Hull, where we shopped and ate and then went on our way again, getting more and more excited every instant. Tumbled nearly on top of Dawson and squeezed into the bus somehow. As we passed Mrs White's cottage, she appeared at the window and clapped her hands with joy at seeing us. At the turn to Davis's, there were all our boys, who on seeing us set off full tilt for the top gate, tumbling over each other on the way. A regular congregation now appeared in sight, all the schoolchildren and some women were waiting to see us. The gate was surmounted by a Union Jack, the children scattered flowers under the horses' feet, and as we again passed through the ancestral portal a cheer was raised from the assembled multitude. A merry peal of bells was struck up, and thus we drove down the approach, feeling very much as if we must have all been just married. Henry, much grown, rushed to open the gate and the bus stops. We are directly in the embraces of Tye [?], and I, getting tired of being wondered at for my height, escaped to the drawing-room and from thence up the stairs to our rooms, feeling perfectly frantic with delight. How we rushed down the passages and all about, making as much row as we could; then down to the garden where Bess was already hugging dirty Nettle [*a dog?*]. Nearly leapt the brook with joy while the waterfall went about its business very placidly, looking too busy to take any notice of us. O it was so nice going to bed at Home, that long-deserved haven, only we wished that Jin had been with us, she having stopped in London with Fanny to go with her to ---- [?].

Kilnwick, June 28, Saturday

I woke! A faint rippling sound came from the waterfall; a sunbeam or two peeped in at the window; the sparrows were chirping in the ivy. Over my head were the old red curtains, and round me the well-known furniture of baby years. How comfortable I did feel to be sure. But all the unpacking had to be done, and soon my room was in a state of utter confusion from which I didn't recover till night. Such delicious old treasures as we discovered in our cupboards, and all the morning passed in examining them. In the afternoon, we all went and stuffed. How nice it was to stuff again mid strawberry beds. The terrace next attracted us, and then we separated and did lots of village. I had my key with me and made use of it, which was very comfortable. The feeling of quiet and content in being at home is delicious, and we came to the conclusion that no mountain scenery is prettier than Kilnwick, with its green fields and trees and little brooks and lovelinesses in which it abounds. May this content last.

Kilnwick, June 29, Sunday

Had Mr Jennings in the morning and Mr Evans in the afternoon, who we didn't admire. We were glad that we had Mr Jennings as there was the H.C. I sat in my old corner, but felt other than I used to be. Our schoolchildren were delighted to have us back, and overwhelmed us with flowers and were as good as gold all the time. We all adjourned to the terrace after Church and had music in the evening.

Kilnwick, June 30, Monday

I wrote to Evelyn in the morning, and in the afternoon Bess and Cis and I trudged off to Bracken to old Tomlinson where we made Cis do all the talking. We did enjoy hopping over the stiles, except one where Bess hopped so high that she nearly cracked her ankles. The Wilmots called sometime, but Fanny seemed quite afraid, of Cis and me especially, and not at her ease; quite the contrary. She was just the same as ever in looks: very pretty etc. I cannot find anything to fill up this page so must shut up.

Here Ends the Journal as a daily routine, but Octavia goes on to write this:

Part Two
A Small Episode in My Life Written from Recollection

The scene commences with a boy looking over a photograph

book. The creature so engaged is tall, slight and nice-looking, aged 23, as yet whiskerless except with a few straggling bits of down which are tenderly cherished and pulled every morning to see if they are grown. The photograph of a young lady arrests his attention. "Who is this?" says he to his sister. "That! O that's Octavia Grimston," she replied. "That's just the kind of girl I should like to marry," said Rowley. "I wonder whether I shall ever see her."

His wonderment was destined to come to pass, for a note soon after arrived inviting his sister, Una Money, to stay at Kilnwick for a fortnight, which was accepted, but there being a mess about the trains she missed the right one and Rowley had to bring her all the way to Kilnwick himself, on which he made this comment: "I'm quite sure it is my fate bringing me to Yorkshire to see that sweet girl Octavia. It must be my fate to marry her."

When he got to Kilnwick he was asked to stay for a few days, which he did, and on Una's asking him what he thought of all of us, he answered: "They are all very nice, I think, but I like Octavia much the best, she has such a heavenly expression and is so nice."

As this was the last that Una would see of Rowley for some time, I used to take care to let them walk alone together, but Una pressed me so much always to walk with them that I did, and she told me afterwards that he whispered to her, "Get Octavia to come out with us, she's a nice girl."

I was not the least aware that he liked me till he went away, when Una told me, also that he wished he had £500 a year and he would soon go at it. I now thought that I should never see him again, and was much amused at what Una told me, but this little story had a sequel.

Alex [*Octavia's brother*] and Una happening to like each other, I had to do the part of bridesmaid, and for that purpose went down to Malvern with Bess and Walter and took up our abode at the Imperial Hotel on Tuesday, Oct 27, 1863 [*when Octavia was*

18 years old]. Next morning we all adjourned to Goodrest where we found Loo and Addy and Aunt Vin and Minnie Money and Aunt Mary and Uncle Oswald and everybody, in fact. Loo and Addy met us at the door and Loo pulled me into the drawing-room saying, "Come along, Rowley is longing to see Miss Ocky."

There was a titter all round the room when we met, and such a squeeze of the claw as I got, which was not his usual mode of shaking hands with other people. Soon a walk was proposed, and we all set out. There was Walter, Addy, Alex, Una, Bess, Loo, me, Minnie and Rowley, and the wicked Loo stuck me next to Rowley. We all went down the street arm in arm and it was very odd how my companion pressed my arm which was in his. We charged everyone we met, including a young ladies' school who looked much amused at us, for we looked and were rather wild. Presently, half the party said they must go home, so away they went and we continued our ramble and at last declared we must have a donkey ride. Up rushed Rowley to the donkey stand, brought down 4 donkeys, made me have the best one and off we set, had a race down to Goodrest and cantered up and down the road for the benefit of the others. Mine being the best, of course, always gained it.

In the evening we all met at Stokefield, where Aunt Una and Aunt Ellen were, and had great fun. There was Janey Onslow there too, in fact all the bridesmaids. We played games and had forfeits. My forfeit was what they called a "bouquet", namely I had to go out of the room and each person chose a flower and I had to say what I would do with them. "What will you do with a white rose?" said Aunt Vin. "Pull it to pieces," said I. What will you do with a myrtle? "Wear it," said I, at which there was a burst of laughter as the myrtle happened to be Rowley and he gave me such a grateful smile for it.

Next day was the wedding, and in the evening a dance to which we all came, and Bess and I had as much as ever we cared for. Among others, Rowley engaged me for a valse, but the stupid boy mistook the one and danced with somebody else. Of course, I did the same, but I watched him to see what he looked like when he remembered it. Suddenly I saw him start and look ashamed of himself, and a despairing expression came over his face while he looked as if he was in for it and cast a furtive glance at me to see if I had thought of it. I looked all offended dignity and went on waltzing. When we stopped he came up to me. "Well, Mr Money, you've done it," says I. "Oh, but I'm so very, very sorry but I quite forgot," said he. "Do forgive me this once and promise me another gallop." "I don't think I shall," I said. "Look what I've done to your name which you wrote on my card," showing him how I had crossed it out with two strokes and written somebody else instead! "Oh, Octavia," said he, looking pleadingly at me. "I know I don't deserve forgiveness, but really I'm sorry and I'll never do it again. Do forgive this once and don't call me 'Mr Money' again." He hated to be called 'Mr Money'. "Well, are you really very sorry?" said I. "Yes, I really am," said he. "Will you never do it again?" said I. "No, I never will," said he. "Then I'll forgive you this time," said I. "Thank you so much," said he. "Now which dance will you give me?" "Well, this one," I said, pointing to a gallop, for I wanted immensely to dance with him, for he danced so very nicely and quietly.

So we had our gallop, and he tried in every way to atone for his wickedness by fanning me when I was hot, etc, and many little attentions. He put on my cloak when I went away, and gave me such a squeeze. O my!

Next day we all met again for a walk. Walter, Addy, Bess, Minnie, Loo, Rowley and I and…… no I made a mistake, that was next day. I forgot what we did, unless we spent the afternoon at Goodrest. In the evening we all met at Mrs Gordon's where there were to be theatricals. Rowley, Aunt Vin, Minnie and a lot of other people acted, and very well they did it too. Between the scenes Rowley used to come in and sit between Loo and me and people played and sang.

Now Bess, during the day, had told me I must be cold to Rowley for he was getting too spooney, so I resolved I would be so when he came and sat between us. I didn't laugh and talk as I used to do with him, which he very soon noticed. "Octavia," said he, "you are grumpy tonight. What's the matter?" "No, I'm not a bit," says I. "Well, something has gone wrong I'm sure," said he, "for you are not yourself." "Well," said I, "perhaps that's true, for something has bothered me rather."

However, I then tried to be amusing, but I felt very miserable indeed, and it was a great effort. Then people bothered me to sing that at last I said I would, but not having my music with me I suddenly broke down in the middle and couldn't go on, on which people all began to clap to encourage me.

Ugh! How horrid I felt, and my tune came back into my head and I went on to the end and then sneaked off to my place with a sort of wild desperate feeling as if I didn't care a bit, for I was very miserable, on which they stuffed me with a lot of wine which made me much better, for I suspect that I was akin to fainting if the truth were known, what with the hot room and everything. Rowley took me in to supper and stuffed me tremendously and tried in every way to make me jolly again. I was so glad when we came home, o so glad.

I felt very seedy and faintified next morning but got better afterwards. We all made an expedition to the top of the Worcestershire Beacon. Rowley took possession of my umbrella and carried it for me. We all got on donkeys at the donkey stand and had tremendous fun, only Rowley was in such a fright whenever my donkey went rather near the edge of the path, lest I should be rolled over, and insisted going there himself instead, which I thought was rather nice of him.

When we got to the top there was such a wind that we couldn't stand hardly, and it was quite impossible attempting to keep on our hats or cloaks, so we buried them in a hole and rushed about without them. Addy tried to keep on her hat but it blew off and the elastic got so tight round her throat that she was nearly strangled. I tried to rush to the rescue, and was nearly rolled over down the hill, on which a long spidery being flew to the rescue, seized me in his arms and pulled me to a sheltered part, declaring he had saved my life for I was on the point of rolling down to the bottom of the hill.

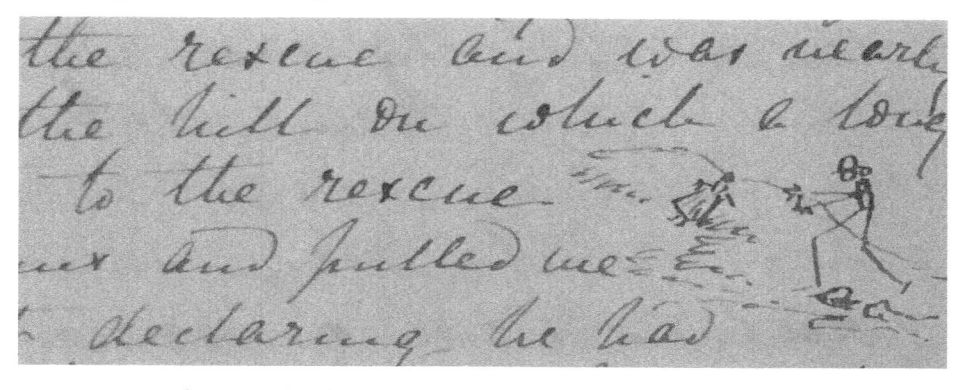

Walter and Minnie now set off arm in arm, in spite of the wind, and looking like wild people of the woods, racing all over the hill.

Rowley and Loo and I did the same, while the soberer ones remained in the hole, and finally we discarded the donkeys and rushed down the hill again, having many chases after refractory hats and a great deal of laughing.

On the way Minnie suddenly stopped, clasped her hands and exclaimed, "Oh, I do believe I've LOST MY HEART! Have I lost my heart? Oh, what shall I do?" We all burst out laughing, thinking most probably she *had* lost her heart as she and Walter had been flirting like anything, but she meant a gold heart she wore round her neck, which however was found to be still there.

We parted company at the corner of Graham Road, but

Rowley would insist on shaking hands with us all, tho we were to meet again at Goodrest in two hours time, I suspect for the object of having a certain hand in his for a few seconds.

A jolly evening we had, but we had to come home tolerably early as it was Saturday night. We intended to be quiet on Sunday, so we were amusing ourselves having some sacred music in the hotel when in walks Addie, Loo and <u>Rowley</u> to see if we would go for a walk with them and go to evening service instead of afternoon. So, we couldn't help ourselves, and off we set with them, giving up the hope of a quiet Sunday.

There being rather a hill after leaving the hotel, Walter made Addie take his arm, on which Rowley made me do the same, but as I had an objection to being seen *comme ça* going through the town, I pretended my cloak wouldn't sit properly and took away my arm, so for a bit he contented himself with carrying my umbrella.

Presently we came to a steeper hill in a less frequented part of the town, so says he, "Octavia, I'm sure you're tired. You look pale. I wish you would take my arm again." So I couldn't refuse, and he declared that I couldn't go as fast as the others, so walked very slow indeed to the top of the hill so that by that time the others were far on in front.

Thinks I to myself, "Well if you <u>will</u> have me alone it most likely is my only chance of talking good to you, and I should like to find out how you are getting on, my dear sir, so I attacked him.

He seemed to be pretty comfortable, tho he said he once had not been, but did not seem inclined to talk about himself at all, so I left off and contented myself with talking moral instead. We talked about Allegories and nature and all sorts of nice things, and about getting up the hill of life, etc.

Presently I said, "I suppose you are going away tomorrow." "No," said he, "I'm not." "Why not?" said I, "for surely you did intend to go on Monday to Kilnwick with Aunt Ellen." "Yes, I did," said he, "but I've changed my mind." "How you do change," I said.

"Then when are you going?" "I expect I'm going next Saturday," he answered. "You go on Friday, don't you?" "Yes," I said. "Well, I don't want to go just yet till you go," he said. "What an odd creature you are," said I. "You're always changing." "No, I don't change in general, only this once," he replied. "I was very unhappy last night because I thought I had done something to offend you, but I'm happier this morning." "I wasn't a bit offended with you," I said. "It was only something that bothers me a wee bit." "Well, I'm glad of that," he said. "I was so afraid I had done something to displease you." "Well, you needn't think so again," I said.

All this time he was squeezing my arm tremendously, and was looking so tenderly at the creature beside him that I began to be a wee bit in a fright. Loo had long ago rushed on with the others on some pretence, and he kept pulling me back and making me walk slow while I was trying to pull him on. At last I said, "How far the others are on in front. Hadn't we better join them?" "Well, there's no reason why we should, unless you dislike walking with me." "No, I don't," said I, so on we proceeded and he grew redder and redder and talked in a low, tender tone and kept looking at me very suspiciously, and long pauses ensued and he began clearing his throat as if making up his mind to say something, till at last I grew in a dreadful fright and thought that the only way was to chatter hard and keep all the conversation to myself, so I began about the new college and every kind of commonplace thing I could think of, till at last, to my great relief, the others stopped at the well which we were going to see and we joined them! Rowley heaved a deep, deep sigh and I whispered to Bess, "Well, I am relieved." And when we went back I tacked myself on to Loo and he walked at her other side, not attempting to come round to mine as he usually did, and not one single syllable did the boy utter the whole way, but pretended to have a very bad cold, which certainly had not been apparent before, and his eyes looked suspiciously watery.

On the way, Capt. Tonge joined us and made a little conversation which was much needed. We went straight to evening service at the Abbey, and Rowley's cold continued very bad all the time and also during sacred music at Goodrest where we went afterwards, when the thing we sang was "Thy Will be Done" especially. Poor boy, I felt so very sorry for him!

Next morning, as we were sitting writing, in walks Loo, Addie and Rowley, but instead of a warm shake his hand felt cold and flabby. He didn't look at me, didn't speak to me and seemed quite anxious to be gone again. Thinks I, this is perfectly odious. I can't stand that.

However, that was all we saw of them that day, and next day we went there in the morning and settled with them that they were to come and dine with us at the hotel. This time Rowley was better, but he was busy writing letters and didn't appear much, however I hadn't a horrid cold shake as before, but he was evidently better.

Bye and bye they came to the hotel. There was Addy, Loo, Rowley, Aunt Mary, Uncle Oswald, Bess and Walter. I sat next to the boy at dinner and we were all as jolly as possible, but he treated me more sisterwise than before.

There were all the Gordons there too, and in the evening we sang Christys and I sang, and Lady Bowe, and altogether had tremendous fun. All the inhabitants of the hotel sat and listened, but bye and bye they all hopped off except Lady Bowe, so we proposed having a dance. She offered to play for us and grand fun it was.

At last Aunt Mary said they must go, so away they went. Bye the bye, on Monday I think it was, we shewed them over the hotel, and as we were coming down again I determined to find out from Loo why Rowley was so cold, so says I to her, "I'm glad Rowley is in better spirits than he was yesterday." "Why, did you find out he was unhappy?" asked Loo. "Of course I did," I answered. "I always see everything and I was so sorry he was so miserable." "Do you know it was you that made him so?" said Loo. "For you were so unkind." "I don't think I was," said I, "but let us sit here on the stairs and have it out."

So down we sat on the stairs and says Loo, "You whispered to Bess that you hated walking with him on Sunday." "I didn't," says I. "You're quite mistaken, for it was something entirely different." "And so of course that vexed Rowley," went on Loo, "and he thinks it must be his having forgotten to dance with you the wedding night that you have not forgiven." Says I, "When I say I forgive a thing I do forgive it, and it isn't that a bit that makes me cold to him." "Then it isn't anything that he has done that has vexed you?" "No," said I. "Then look here," says Loo. "When he shakes hands with you going away, just say 'It's all right,' and he will understand." "No, I really can't," says I. "You must tell him."

We then joined the others, and when they went away Loo watched anxiously to see whether I did what she told me. Presently, up comes Rowley. "Goodnight Rowley," I said, at the same time giving a grin to Loo, but not saying 'It's all right'.

Next day we made an expedition to Hereford, carrying off Addie with us, where we met the Huntingfords and Minnie and went to service at the cathedral. We went straight to Goodrest when we came back again and had tea there. Rowley sat next me and appeared quite jolly again and stuffed me so, O dear.

Our last day dawned for our stay at Malvern, and being in a good mood, Bess and I went off to the Martins as a last act of duty, and in the evening we might be seen at Goodrest, listening to a woman playing on a dulcimer.

Loo, Rowley and I sprawled on the sofa till they said why shouldn't we dance. No sooner said than done, and we had a delicious carpet dance and I waltzed a lot with Rowley and other things besides till we were too hot to dance any more, and we agreed that it was much greater fun than the dance on the evening of the wedding. Such a shake of the paw as I got for the last, and they watched us till we were off with many nods and sweet goodbyes and kisses of the claw. So here's an end of 1, 2 and 3: Aunt Vin, and Addieee and the nice boy Rowleeee. Next day we were off to London and saw them no more.

The end of the little episode is only from what I was told, like the beginning, and not from personal experience, so here it is. Instead of going straight home as we intended, we went back into Herefordshire to stay with the Martins and so missed Rowley who was staying at Neswick [*near Driffield, east Yorkshire*] which I was rather sorry for. However, as he was not to leave Yorkshire for a few days there was yet a chance of seeing him when we got home.

So one day we went over to Lund [*also near Driffield*]. "Oh," said Una, I expect Aunt Ellen and Rowley here in a minute." However, when the carriage arrived there was only Aunt Ellen and no Rowley, so when we went away I whispered to Una, "You may tell Rowley when you see him tomorrow that I was sorry he didn't come today, and give him my love," which she did, for he was in very low spirits, but directly he heard it he nearly jumped out of the window with joy and gave her messages yards long to give to me back again. And on bewailing that mothers don't sometimes give their consent to things, Una said, "Well you know my dear boy, if it <u>is</u> to happen it <u>will</u> happen notwithstanding the opposition of all the mothers in Christendom!" which seemed greatly to comfort him. And he told Una that he couldn't the least make out when I liked him or not at Malvern. All messages and intercourse being now stopped, I closed this little story, but I wonder much whether it will ever be continued.

Pasted below this sorry tale of misery and manipulation is a newspaper cutting for the marriage of Rowland E. K. Money of the 3rd Goorkha Regiment to Adelaide Meta Sanderson, daughter of the superintendant of the Peninsula and Oriental Company of Calcutta.

ARTHUR C. VENTRESS

> **MARRIAGES.**
> On the 11th Dec., at St. Stephen's Church, Bareilly, by the Rev. J. Richards, chaplain, ROWLAND E. K. MONEY, Esq., 3d Ghoorka Regt., to ADELAIDE META, second daughter of JOHN PATERSON, Esq., Superintendent Peninsular and Oriental Co., Calcutta.

Part Three

My Visit to Ireland, May 22nd, 1866

I wonder why it is that I care so little to go to Ireland this time. Maybe I shall enjoy it more for not having built castles beforehand. Mama, Jin and I are bound together for the next six weeks, and Ferney is our 1st destination. Our journey was accomplished comfortably, the sea being calm, and I stayed on deck till the sun set, chaperoned by a woman with a terrible brogue, as Jin and Mama went to bed. I liked the passage and amused myself reading and crooning hymns and watching the lights on the sea, and the porpoises so busy turning head over heels, and loth was I to turn in when it got dark. And now we arrive at Ferney, which is not a bit changed since I saw it and its inmates 3 years ago.

Uncle Stuart and Aunt Bessie are staying here, and Uncle S read prayers and expounded so nicely. But there are a few notes in the Ferney chord which jar sadly on strange ears. The groove is narrow and people are plucked and pulled indiscriminately.

The day after we arrived, there being a flower show in Dublin, we went to amuse ourselves there; but first, having time to spare, we went to 10 D'Olier St. I having a fancy for being attacked, went into a corner, and sure enough up comes Miss James, and laying 2 tracts before me asked if I knew them. On me saying I did, she began saying how nice they were and then asked me a personal question at which I chuckled, but finding me pretty satisfactory she did no more catechism, and then I told her who I was and we fraternised.

Next we went to see Frith's picture of the railway station. I liked it very much, but should have liked to examine it by myself for as long as I liked. We met Henry and Bena and with them walked about the Rotunda gardens where the show was held. There were such crowds. I looked much more at the people than the flowers.

We were introduced to Mr Johnson, supposed to be a cousin, and were talking to him when who should appear but John Adair, who said he would come back and dine with us, so he did. He and I went behind the carriage coming from the station, and he took such care of me, putting his coat over my dress to keep it from the dust. He asked us to come to Belgrove, which I should like, but Mama is afraid of Mrs M, and he said "It is so very pleasant to have you among us again," and declared that I was not a bit changed because I still hummed when I was thinking about anything, as I used to do.

A great discussion went on at dinner about Cromwell and his times, which was interesting. There was a good parson, Mr Wallace, came to Church, who gave us such a beautiful discourse on Heb.12 at prayers and prayed so nicely. We hoped John took it in. I think he is more inclined that way than he was, but it is hard to tell.

Somehow Jin and I both feel an unaccountable feeling of discontent, whether from want of employment I don't know, but it is very distressing. I hope I shall get better.

On our last day at Ferney, we got Francy and Rose Trench to come for the afternoon, and after a long croquet game we proposed a read, so ensconcing ourselves on the steps of the arbour we had a very pleasant read in Phil III, but the girls wouldn't give out many ideas. Then leaving them on the way to the train we went to 5 o'clock tea at the Guinesses, where I sang many hymns, then ran home to dress for dinner as Aunt Townshend was coming. Aunt Colley made Mama promise to come back there on her way home, and next day we departed for Carrick.

May 30. At Dublin station we saw a boy of about 19, who Lily declared shook hands exactly like Alfred, and on his turning round his face was so like A's that when he got into our carriage Mama asked him if he was a Trench, and sure enough he was Alfred's brother James, who was also on his way to Carrick, so we all went together, Mama discoursing him all the way.

Uncle Stuart met us at Enniskillen and chose Jin for his companion on the box, and so we arrived at Ennis Castle. George Power was staying there, and Johnny Trench and Janet came to dinner every night.

The day after we arrived, Uncle S took us to see all his Fenian fortifications and his farm and the market house, and finally the Morants. Being market day, we had to go two and two, escorted by our squires, so I had a little talk with James, thus making known to each other what sort of people we each were.

At Hurley House I got Willie alone as we were walking round the garden, and sitting down in a grotto had a long talk. She told me she was dreadfully shaky in the church, and as we needed our bible we escaped to her room and having a little prayer set too at all the puzzling texts. How utterly hopeless it makes one feel, trying to make it plain to others. It is so entirely in His hands to give the light and wisdom needed. It is comforting, though, to feel so helpless, for His strength is made perfect in weakness.

We didn't like to stay very long, so showing me some texts which I was to think over, we joined the others, and when I came home I had a long read to get it clear and Lily helped me too very much. The Morants came to dinner, and all the evening we played at letters spelling words and I was so bored - O my! - for I had set my heart on having either a talk with Willie or James, who is also shaky, and couldn't manage it.

Next morning (Friday June 1) an expedition to Castle Blaney was proposed, which I instantly joined in voting for, though the day was not propitious as it began with a drizzle. But as it kindly cleared by 12 1/2, off we went, taking Willie with us.

There were 3 carriages, no. 1 with Aunt B and Lily, no. 2 Uncle St, Mama, Willie and James, no. 3, a car containing Johnny, me, Jin and George Power, and a pleasant drive we had. I had a very pleasant talk with Johnny and told him some of Mrs Grant's stories.

We drove all through the Castle Blaney grounds, such a delicious avenue and a winding road through a wood carpeted with bluebells, with views of the lake and its islands all the way along. O so lovely. Then we betook ourselves to a sort of little temple on a green hill where we left the carriages, and after demolishing sandwiches and biscuits and roasting ourselves at a fire, we young ones all sallied forth into the wood which grew more and more lonely the further we went, and at last took up our position in a shed full of logs which made capital seats. And there in a ring we sat and pulled out our bibles, which we had brought with us, and had a read together in Luke. But it was not very satisfactory, I thought, for we read a long chapter, and most of us were too frightened to speak much and didn't go as much into it as I should have liked. After this we sang "One There Is" and then, thinking the elders might be wondering where we were, we turned towards the rendezvous and found the Uncle Stuart had gone to fetch a boat and was coming to take us over the lake.

We wondered what George Power thought of our proceedings in the log house, as he does not care much for those sort of things himself, like most other boys of his age. Lily wasn't allowed to go in the boat, lest she should catch cold, so we little children, with Uncle Stuart to take care of us lest we should get into mischief, tumbled into it and rowed to the island where we disported ourselves and walked and talked pleasantly the while. Such a delicious place as it was, with the carpet of ferns and bluebells and the trees so thick that it was almost dark, jolly place for a morbid person to meditate in.

Then we rowed to the house and after looking over it got into the carriages for our homeward journey. This time we arranged ourselves differently, Johnny and Lily being together on the car and James and I. He and I had a long talk about the Church, but tho I gave all my little reasons and persuasions he talked me down, for he seemed to have regularly thought about it all and I couldn't make much impression.

Then Johnny proposed having a hymn, so I struck up, and we kept some way behind the other so as not to be heard and had many pleasant hymns and the boys grew much less shy of us and we got on capitally. They invited us to 5 o'clock tea at their house the next day, which we settled to do, and Johnny tried to upset James and me into a hedge but couldn't manage it.

We enjoyed ourselves <u>immensely</u> and were quite sorry to get home where we didn't arrive till near 8 pm. The boys came to dinner, and Uncle J declared he would carry me off to Glenveagh with him this summer, as he intends going there and saw how I wanted to see it. Mama gave her consent, but I dare not reckon upon it, it would be too pleasant.

We were very tired so went to bed early to recruit exhausted nature, and now having written you up to the present time, my journal, we are going into Uncle S's room to sing hymns. All the boys came up too and we'd a regular little meeting, but I didn't enjoy it much. I do like hymns in tune, I don't like arguments or deep discussions on prophecy.

In the evening we went down to Inver Lodge at 5 o'clock and

all had a read together. Mama and Aunt B and Georgie Power were out driving, so we going over had it all to ourselves and very pleasant it was. We read, and were not quite so shy as in the log house. Then the elders joined us and we had tea and great fun and went over the house. Johnny has a skull just opposite his bed, a pleasant spectacle when one awakes.

On Sunday we had only morning service, but there was the Communion. It was nice so many of us together, but I was sorry James didn't stay for it. In the afternoon we all went to the lake and read, but it was too argumentative, not what one could feed upon at all. I'm sorry this is our last night. We go tomorrow to Kilbeg. Monday Willie came, and Louie, and we sat on the terrace and talked. The boys came to luncheon and I got James's photo and then off we went.

June 4. The Kells [*County Meath*] people met us half way and we got there in time for dinner. It is not so very primitive a place as I expected, but I think they were smartened up for us. Sally is very pretty I think. I can't write all the accounts of Kells. I'm Lazy.

O dear, it was such formidable work at prayers. We all had to read a verse in turn, and I was so afraid of coming to hard names and tumbling over them. I sang all Maudie's and my things, which they delighted in, and we had many hymns every night, and I liked the little bits of good talk poking in in every conversation. It seemed as if the thoughts were in the right place. Sally and I had delicious little reads together every night in her room, which I thoroughly enjoyed, and the last night we'd a little prayer. She said I helped her very much, which made me very happy. Robby came 2 days before we left, and he and I had a nice talk out riding one day. I expect Rochfort will be a very different life from this.

We left Kells on Saturday 9th and stopped in Dublin to see Fanny O'Hara, who was very glad to see us but she's very much changed, looks older and sadder and not so pretty. Having some time to spare, we went by train to Raheny [*a northern suburb of Dublin*] hoping to see Alfred and Netta who were staying with

Mrs Trench, but they'd gone into Dublin for the whole day. Stupid people! It was so disappointing. We saw only Mrs Trench, Agnes and Helen, had luncheon there and then went off to Mullingar. We thought of the little scene in the train as we went along and looked curiously at the Mullingar station, which we knew so well by hearsay. The Tottenham's carriage was waiting, so we bundled into it and got in time to Rochfort, but our boxes hadn't come yet so we had to come down to dinner in our travelling frocks, which was not comfortable as a lot of people were staying in the house.

I looked well at all the people at dinner and made up my mind about them all, not rightly though, as I afterwards found. Two very pretty girls were opposite me. O, thought I, you look worldly, fashionable, clever girls. I wonder whether we shall be able to talk to you. Then there were two brothers, Langley and Augustine Lefroy. One looked gentlemanlike and nice, the other vulgar and conceited, and a Miss Caulfield, whom I didn't like the look of: not very ladylike and ugly withal, thought I.

Having thus made up my mind about my neighbours, I did my best to talk to the man who was next me who had come to dine. After dinner Kate Molesworth (the eldest of the pretty girls) and I got together in a window and she astonished me very much by being so unreserved. I tried to meet her halfway and be unreserved too, but somehow I could not be so to a person of whom I knew nothing. She was a great chatterpie and I liked her very much. In person she was short and slight, very pretty figure, woolly auburn hair, inclining to red, done up fashionably in many puffs, pretty hazel eyes and good features. Gracie, the younger one, has a figure like little Willie's, very graceful, her face is quite lovely, I think; very large dark blue eyes and long lashes and pencilled eyebrows and lovely clear complexion and wee mouth. Her hair is darkish brown, drawn quite off her face and puffs behind. Rather a sad little face when quiet. She told me she was 21, 5 months older than me.

When the gentlemen came in we had some music. Kate sang

first, then me and then a duet between the two girls. I sang The Watchman and then Redeemed which people liked much, and on my saying to Gracie I had no others in my head but sacred ones, she said she liked them so much the best. O, thought I, that looks nice. I wonder if you are good after all. Both the Lefroys seemed very much in love with Grace, we thought, but I shouldn't have liked to be quite so familiar with them myself as the girls were.

Later in the evening Grace, Mr Augustine (the nice one) and I were behind the piano. I was looking over her song book, saw Resignation and said how I liked it. "Ah," she said, "I cannot bear to sing it now, hardly even to look at it since my brother died. It was such a great sorrow to us, but the Lord sends strength with sorrow. I always think," she went on, "how differently sorrows are taken by a converted person and those who are not Christians. It makes them so much less if we can see His love in them, and if we are at perfect peace with Him. O what peace it is, it indeed passeth all understanding. I could never have gone through all I have had to bear, before I was a Christian." I heard a growl from Mr Augustine. "How absurd of you saying you weren't a Christian." "No," said Grace, "I was not a Christian till two years ago. I was not worthy to bear that sacred name." "I don't believe you've had so much sorrow as you seem to say," growled he again. "I've had such sorrow," she answered again, "that it nearly killed me. I can hardly bear to think of it now, but it only makes us cling closer to our Saviour."

In this strain she went on for a long time, talking so nicely and seeming so happy. It made me so glad to find out she was good and she said her sister was the same. And she didn't seem to care a bit talking before people, not a bit ashamed of saying how much she cared for it, which I admired in her very much. I was quite in love with her and she said she knew we cared for good things, for Mrs Tot had told her so and her heart leapt for joy when she heard it, but Kate and she were always talking about their hearts and their conversation was so fanciful and rather romantic that at first it gave one the impression that there was more outward show than inward reality in her religion.

The next day was Sunday and we 3 children went off early to practise the harmonium. Mr Langley said he would come with us, but was ordered not by Mrs Tot, so he sulked. A Mr Adams preached a beautiful sermon on the "Secret of the Lord" but I was sorry to hear afterwards that he was not very good. Grace and I came home behind the carriage, and how Mr Augustine did muffle her up and tuck her in at the risk of his own neck, for he was standing on top of the wheel all the time, and stayed there all the longer because she begged him not.

When we got home, Grace proposed that we should go and meet the walkers, so we did, and she said Mr Augustine was good tho' shy and she had delicious talks with him. When we met them I took Miss Caulfield and left Gracie and Mr A together to walk home. I hope they made good use of their time.

In the afternoon we all went different ways. Grace would go alone, Miss C and Kate went together; and Jin and I, after inspecting the garden, set off for the cottage at the end of the wood. But I got tired, so turned into the wall by the lake and sat there and read for a long time, very glad to escape from all the people, for one must talk so much rubbish with a large party, or at least one <u>does</u>. We had lots of hymns in the evening.

On Monday morning, <u>Grace and I had another delicious talk</u> behind the piano, and I think the romantic language she uses is only habit and at any rate she's far better than I am. She read me a beautiful letter from a Scotch friend of hers. We went all over Belvedere, the place next to Rochfort by the lake, and got the gardener to give us many flowers, making Grace ask for them, for nobody could resist her pretty face.

Some of us came back in the boat. I acted as chaperone, not a very severe one, for I allowed Mr Augustine and Grace to flirt all by themselves at one end of the boat while Langley, <u>Kate and I</u> sat at the other. When we landed, feeling very disinclined to come in, we went for a walk in the wood to gather ferns, and great fun we had.

We were very uproarious at dinner. I got next Kate and we cut waterlilies and caterpillars out of oranges, and cracked Philippine nuts, over which Mr Augustine and Kate had a fight. She wouldn't take a Philippine and left it on her plate, and after dinner, when the gentlemen came in, he took hold of her hand and put the Philippine nut in it, at which she got very angry and tossed it into the fire. She's a very nice girl, we like her immensely, but don't like Miss C, though she's odd and amusing.

Next day, in the afternoon, Gracie, Jin and I had a walk by the lakes, and a great deal of talk. She's a regular little Plymouth Sister in heart, has been at their Communion, etc, though she does not approve of all their ways. She told us about her family, how her mother is so good and works, and they have meetings in their kitchen and in the cottage, and about her own conversion. They are so open and unreserved. She told us she was engaged once, but her creature turned Plymouthy and it wasn't allowed to come off.

A Mr MacGill came to stay in the house. We'd great fun at dinner again after which we had music, and Langley tacked himself on to Gracie for the whole evening and talked in tender and mysterious tones.

I overheard a bit of a good talk going on. Grace thought she had snubbed Mr Langley, so the night before had tried to make up for it which certainly succeeded, for he's more in love than ever though she can't bear him. Mr Augustine has quite left the field to his brother, rather nice and unselfish of him.

Wednesday. This was the Lefroys' last day and they would stick in the drawing-room all the morning. At last we got Mr McGill and Mr Augustine to go out fishing, but nothing would induce Mr Langley to go away from Grace, so I got tired of them and went and sat under a tree to read. Kate had some flowers to dress, so while she was doing them, up comes Mr Langley and said, "Miss Molesworth, can you give me any hope about your sister, do you think?" "Not the slightest," said Kate, "for she does not like you well enough." So he said, "I thought she didn't like me from the first," and then looked very miserable for the rest of the morning. Poor man, I pitied him for being so unhappy.

The afternoon was spent in croquet, and when it rained we blew bubbles, and Mr Augustine gave me a lesson in billiards till it was time for them to go, but they dawdled till the last minute. At last it was time for us to dress, so we all bid goodbye and were going upstairs. Kate and Grace were the last, and looking back I caught them having another good shake of the claw. I heard afterwards that they said, "Do let us have one more shake before we part, for we have been so happy together." I mean the Lefroys said it. It seemed quite lonely without them, and we found it hard to talk at dinner. Mr Macgill was the only gentleman. He's very nice, like Major Goff, not extra good I should think, but a pleasant man. Ghost stories filled up the evening. Mr MacGill went away next morning, but said he should see us again in the Queens County [*now County Laois*].

Thursday was our last day at Rochfort, and a very pleasant one, for we 4 girls walked over to Bloomfield, intending to meet Miss Caulfield, but didn't, which I didn't grieve over. I had Grace all the time and Jin had Kate. They told us lots of nice stories - one about Mr Augustine. He wanted once to get to know a certain girl very much, and his only chance was by going to a fancy ball. Now, he had given up balls, but however he went and got introduced to the girl. During their conversation she said, "Do you know I have been so disappointed this evening? I heard you were religious, and I thought how nice to find an officer like that, there are so few of them. But I find I was mistaken, for you have been talking to me like anyone else and are no better than the rest of them." Mr Augustine felt quite sick at heart and left the ball immediately, resolving never to go to another, and he never did.

Another story was about the religious Miss Orr. Grace said Mr Langley had told her he had overheard a talk between her and me, and it had made him want so to be good if only he could get anyone to lead him, and asked her if she would. But she answered that it was in the hands of a higher power to do that. She then told me many instances of answers to prayer, and we had a delicious talk which helped me much. We sang a hymn as we came home. In the evening we turned into the hall and played dumb crambo [*similar to charades*] and Magic Music and the Cradle and proverbs and were quite wild.

This is our last night. The girls and we have got to kissing and Christian names. I copied "Redeemed" for Grace as she liked it so much, and next morning we departed with much regret, having enjoyed ourselves immensely. I wonder if we shall ever meet those sweet little girls again on earth. In Dublin we called on old Mrs MacGill and there found the son, so we talked over Rochfort and the happy days there. We also called on Mrs Burke who wants us to stay with her, but we don't want to. Ballantyre is now our abode.

June 15, Friday. Myrie came over just after we arrived and asked me to go to her for a night or two, so I'm going, I believe, from Tuesday to Thursday, as I want to know Isa. We went on Saturday to Mrs White's of Killakee [*House*] to a 4 o'clock ----. Such a crowd. We met Gussy Power there and Myrie, Bena, Lily, Maria Trench and the Kirkpatricks, but didn't enjoy it much. I wish I could have Aunt J to myself, I could get on so much better. Now I must go to bed, so goodnight my journal.

Well! I went to Mr Merrion's, and they were very kind to me, and I had a long talk with Isa out in the garden one morning and told her many stirring-up stories. I sang all my sacred things many times, and had little talks with Myrie occasionally. I hope my visit was not wholly useless.

On Friday we went to Glennalyre, taking Millicent on our way. All are at home except Thomas, but he comes back on Sunday, having gone away to fish. Dear old place, how it brings back the wild, happy days 3 years ago, and they do spoil me so here.

On Saturday we went to the Malards to croquet, where were some little fast girls who smoke, and some officers. John Adair came to dinner and we sang in the evening. I pretended to be very wild and jolly but was very miserable at some things Myrie told me about John, which seem as if he was getting worse instead of better. When will the creature be good? It is so hard to have any faith about him and it seems so incongruous being jolly with him as if all was right. We sat on the hall door steps in the evening, and I told all their fortunes, and John was rather in a nice mood. They want me to talk to the boys, but how to manage it I don't know, for I never get them alone. I sang lots of sacred things, which were liked.

Thomas came on Sunday. The Owl made me very unhappy, it was so miserable, not a bit like what it used to be, never joins in the laughter and fun going on, but runs away by itself and looks wretched. Lizzie and I were great friends. I like that girl. On Sunday evening I had been singing the Sacred Heart. J.S. was sitting beside me, and then I sang "A Little While" [*by Horatius Bonar*] ending with "Beyond Remembering and Forgetting" "That's not true," says J.S. "I never thought of that," said I. "It is not true for I believe we shall remember each other perfectly there." "That was not what I meant," said J. S. "But how can we be beyond remembering and forgetting when the thought of our sins is to make us miserable forever?" Says Fanny, "Why, you sound as if you thought you were going to hell." "Well! and isn't that true?" "O," said I, "You are forgetting the last part of the Sacred Heart," singing it over in a low voice again. How one wishes one could put into people a bit of one's own peace.

Dear, dear, there's a deal of misery in the world. Aunt Bess is miserable because Freddy is gone to fight the Fenians in America [*The Fenian Brotherhood made raids into Canada from the US in April 1866*] and because Henry is to go to India in a few days. Fanny is miserable for her twin's sake, and I'm miserable because everybody else is miserable. Such is life. In other ways, neither life nor I are at all unhappy. I'm perfectly cracked and go on in a very mad way, except when Owlet is present, but the girls say my being jolly will make me have more influence with the boys if I get a chance of putting in a word.

Fanny and I had a long talk under a tree, and she likes me and thinks I understand her, so I have power in that direction, and I'm very fond of her too. I can say some things to her which I can't to others about these same miseries. But I have a strong conviction that they will get right some day, and the joy will be the greater for the sorrow beforehand. I think that conviction is given to one when the answer to one's prayers is on the road. It's a curious fact that in reading with Mama we happened to read Mark II to get right with the day, and the 24th verse ["*Therefore I tell you, whatever you ask in prayer, believe that you have received it, and it will be yours.*"] came so wonderfully like an answer to what I'd been asking for, making the request turn from the minor to the major key. We go out after dinner every night, and each time I hope to get somebody alone, but am each time disappointed. I had Henry alone for 1/2 an hour one morning, but somehow I didn't know how to do it, for he talked so much about his life in Bermuda, and so that chance passed by neglected.

There is going to be a dance on Thursday here, and the boys are out all day asking officers to come to it. We go on Friday. I don't like the thought of this dance a bit, but though it was left mostly to my decision, the boys were so anxious for it that I voted for it too, hoping I was not wrong.

On Tuesday we all went, except the boys, to Monasterevin to the moors where John Adair came too, and some other people, and we went boating down the river [*Barrow*] and were very happy. Another day we went all over Belgrove, delicious place it is. Another day to Portarlington and Emo Park, where Myrie and I sat in the garden and I regaled her with Mr Grant's stories.

Letitia de Voeux came for an afternoon to Glenmalyre, a jolly girl and very good they say. I wonder privately whether she will ever be Mrs Thomas. Somehow I hope not, for she's not pretty or *distingué* enough, though perhaps I oughtn't to mind that for she's so good.

The party night arrived. Aunt Bessy had spent her night in tears about Henry, so was not up to much. There were great preparations going on all day and Liz and I practised quadrilles till my musical nerves were strung painfully tight. I got up at 4 1/2 that morning to make a tarlatan body for my dress, and worked hard all day, just finishing it in time.

Frank Saunderson and two girls, Mimsa and Anne Moore came to dinner, as they were to stay over the night for it. I liked Frank very much, and Anne Moore is very nice indeed too, and good withal. Thomas and Henry got me some lovely waterlilies for my hair, which when done up with blue ribbon looked uncommonly pretty though I says it. I had a very pleasant talk with John Adair about happiness before the dancing began, but I never saw him all the rest of the evening except just to bid him goodbye.

I danced the 1st and last dances with Thomas, and having him alone on the approach tried to talk a little bit, but he didn't seem to like it so I shut up. I danced the whole evening without stopping, except when parading on the approach, which was quite as good. Twice with Charly, and had a long talk with him which he liked very much. Once with Frank, and paraded for ages between the gates and got on very well. Twice with a Captain Airey, who was very nice and sensible and who liked me and bid me a tender farewell at the end, hoping to see me some day in Yorkshire. Once with Captain Lee, once with Harry Moore, once with Capt. XXX, once with Henry and tried to talk to him, but he was so wild and enjoying himself so much that he was not in a mood for it, so I couldn't say much. I believe there were some more, but I forget them.

Captain Airey, Henry and I had such a funny talk on the Ottoman one time. We began about parsons going to balls, as there was one there dancing, and had an interesting talk about them though we disagreed very much. Then said Captain Airey, "Do you know, a lady startled me so much the other day at a dinner party. She turned round and said suddenly, 'Salvation is very pleasant.'"

I thought to myself, that's the worst of not using tact in speaking to people, but I tried to say a wee word as the talk had turned on that subject.

I enjoyed myself so much I felt very happy at having been allowed to do a little good. I hope they were not my own words, so that they may work and bear fruit. I was not in bed till 5, when it was broad daylight, and I was quite tired having got up so early too.

Everybody there seemed to enjoy themselves immensely, and some said they would have walked all the way from the Curragh to come to such a pleasant evening. It was so delicious parading, the moon was full and it was so warm and the stars out, just the time for quiet talks with people.

I liked escaping from the dancing to the beautiful quiet nature outside, it suited better with my feelings. My Owlet seemed rather better, dear old bird. It likes me very much I believe, and so do I it. Bye the bye, of course the Owl was better at night because night suits an owl's feelings better than the broad sunshine. O for the light inside to be so great that the sunshine may appear quite dark compared to it. We must wait and pray for the dawning, for surely it will come as surely as the sunrise that night eclipsed the moon and stars.

Next morning after breakfast I packed, and then all we girls with the Moores had a read in the schoolroom, in the middle of which up rushed Henry to say the carriage was coming round and he'd been looking for me all over the place. Off I rushed to get on my things, and ran down to bid hasty goodbyes and jumped into the carriage leaving them all disconsolate on the door step. They want me very much to come back after Wykeham, but I'm afraid it's not practicable, though no one knows how much I should like it. The will is not wanting.

Well, I've enjoyed my Wykeham visit too very much. They tried so hard to make it pleasant for us. Helen and I were great friends and had many nice talks together and a very pleasant read in the garden. We went down the river barge-fashion one day with the Crosthwaites and Newtons and they stayed in the evening and we paced on the gravel and I told ghost stories. Helen wants me to stay in Ireland and wait for Cis coming over and live with her at Burrace. Ma says nay, but Pa is on my side [*presumably Helen's father, as Octavia's was dead by this time*]. I intends to beg.

Now we are at Trimliston, having been at Wykeham from June 29 to July 3. People intend going to Dublin today, I believe, to St Patrick's service if we can. I wonder what's happening at Glenmalyre today. I feel somehow as if Owlet was happy. What would I give to know if it were really the case?

We went to St Patrick's and enjoyed it very much, as also to St Vincent's Hospitals which we were shown over by a man, such an ugly one. There was a poor man dying in the ward and receiving extreme unction from the priest. It made us very sad. Then we went to see Rose Trench, who was sick. The Trimliston people were very kind and did everything they could to amuse us. I liked the twins and got on very well with them.

From them we went to the Burkes for two nights. I dreaded being there very much, for I found Philippa, the daughter, so uninteresting and hard to get on with when we called there, but really it was not bad at all, for I went with Ulick Burke more than anybody, who was my slave while I was there, a boy about 20, exactly like the Colley's footman but gentlemanlike, who agreed with everything I said whether it was preposterous or not. I had many moral talks but could never manage real good, though I had plenty of opportunity. He informed me that mine was the nature to lead and his to be led and learn.

Philippa really was more talkative when out of hearing of her mother, in fact talked so much when we were alone that I couldn't get a word in of what I wanted. Ulick and Mrs Burke had a fight one night because she wanted Jim to play a thing on the violin which he didn't want to and wouldn't, so I expressed my grief at his conduct next morning. I hope he'll be better next time.

We went with them to the Winter Garden in Dublin to hear a man play on the *Cornet* à *pistons,* Levy by name. It was beautiful, certainly. I saw Langley Lefroy in the distance, but never got near him, which I was sorry for, for it took one back to Rochfort seeing him, and I should have enjoyed a talk over the days there.

We left Milltown Saturday 7th July for Ferney, first going to Dublin to meet Tom, who came up from Enniskillen on purpose and met us in Reynold's Hotel. He told us that Willie had left the E.C. as we feared and said she was so happy in consequence and worked now like anything. Mama was rather knocked up with seeing him and it was not very satisfactory on the whole.

I had such a happy Sunday for my last in Ireland. There was the H.C. and such a nice clergyman very like Chickey White who gave us a delicious sermon about conformity to the world.

A very happy day was that last, and now we depart for home, first being nearly upset in a cab in Dublin and having many misfortunes. Jin had suggested my being left behind as the Glenmalyre people and Chapmans wanted, but Mama wouldn't hear of it, so I go home.

There were lots of people going to America in our steamer, and such crying and hugging and partings as there were, like what one reads of in books. Mama left me on deck in charge of an old woman whom I had a long talk with till 9 o'clock when we subsided downstairs, and in fact I'm at home again and my Irish tour is over and so there's an end of the matter as my impressions of it can hardly be trusted to black and white.

Part Four

A Glimpse into Scotland
September and October 1866

An invitation from the Maxwells came one day for Cis and me to go and visit them at Speddoch, followed quickly by invites from the Grahams of Mossknow and Murrays of Murraythwaite, which after due consideration were accepted, and on the 21st of Sept Cis and I with Campey [*servant?*] were launched on the wide world to sink or swim as we liked.

Thus we arrived at Speddoch and were warmly welcomed by Gertie and Mr Maxwell and an aunt, Miss Sprott, who was staying there. My first impressions of Mr Maxwell were decidedly flattering to him; my second ones were that I was a <u>little</u> afraid of him. He is so clever and makes one feel a great donkey, and as if one knew nothing, and I began to wonder if I should be happy at Speddoch or not. I rather thought <u>not</u> but it remained to be proved.

Miss Sprott was a dear kind old thing with plenty of fun in her, and we liked her very much. Gertie was just the same as ever. Friday was the day of our arrival and on Saturday we drove to the Routin Bridge. Such a lovely waterfall. We clambered down under the bridge to see it. How happy it must be to be able to give people so much pleasure while simply going about its daily business. I'd a nice bit of talk with Miss Sprott as we went, and she was so nice and good, I found, but she goes away on Monday which I'm sorry for.

Sunday I cannot say I much enjoyed. One long Scotch service sitting during the singing, standing at the prayers, and a very long sermon proving the truth of the resurrection.

We had a nice walk in the afternoon to the moor, through the loveliest of lovely glens with ferns and bright moss and winding paths and a little torrent tumbling over stones and banks of overhanging ivy. Then we sat on the moor and sang hymns, and the rest of the day read and had music in the evening. Cis was completely knocked up, and all but fainted next morning. We went to Gribton that day, and Mrs Walker doctored Cis, making her take about a copperful of hot water, which Cis ever since has suggested to me as a remedy for low spirits or any ailment both of body and mind. Gertie says there's a Mr Saunders coming on Tuesday, a barrister and good withal. I do like good people.

So, Mr Saunders did come on Tuesday. In outward appearance 5ft 10 1/2, immensely thick hair almost like a wig, small eyes but other features good, very pleasant merry face and peaceful expression. One could tell he was good. There was a dinner-party that night, and he took me in to dinner and I found him very pleasant to talk to. It is so nice hearing him and Professor Harkness [*probably Robert Harkness, geologist*] and Mr Maxwell discussing deep subjects, they are all so clever. The Professor is staying in the house for 2 days. He's a nice old man, very good about explaining deep things to our small minds. We were sorry when he had to go. Miss Sprott went on Monday, after giving me a commission to make her a tatting cap, which she paid me for, for the benefit of the London Biblewomen.

On Thursday we went to Drumlanrig, the Duke of Buccleugh's place. Mr Maxwell was to meet us there, so Gertie, Cis, I and Mr Saunders went in the carriage. We'd a nice talk in the carriage, found out Mr S. was right, and he told us about work in London and how a lot of young men, and he among them, visited in different parishes and looked after sick people and read with them. It was very interesting hearing about them. We walked about the Drumlanrig gardens, and the hills were lovely, but I was longing to be roaming through the nice woods there are there, instead of being chaperoned by a gardener through the prim, neatly kept gardens.

Our evenings were generally spent in music. They all like our sacred things so much. The days passed quickly by without much adventure till Sunday, our second one in Scotland. We drove to a different church this time, at Trougray, which we liked far better; there was such a nice minister, beautiful prayers and sermon and a pleasant talk we had on the way too, and having had an English service to ourselves at home first, we didn't miss it so much.

In the afternoon we again walked to the moor, establishing Cis on a campstool at the end of the glen while we went on. Mr S. and I went on in front and had a very nice talk on many subjects. It is so pleasant getting new friends who really are earnest about these things. It helps oneself. It was odd that at long prayers that night Mr M. read us a sermon on world [?] which suited so well with our conversation. We liked the way in which Mr S. tried to bring in little good bits at dinner, but all that evening he was evidently very unhappy and we could not make out what was troubling him, giving deep sighs and often lost in thought. He read us a sermon in the evening on "the irreparable past" and sounded so miserable while reading it, poor man, we were quite sorry for him and longed to ask him what was the matter. [*A coded sentence follows - "A hearty shake I got that night," it seems to read, presumably referring to a handshake from Mr Saunders.*]

On Monday we drove off to Blairinnie up in the hills. The cloud on the spirit was still hanging there. We first walked onto the moor to see a lovely view of the Dee and mountains beyond, so nice and blue and misty, reminding one of 'the distant hills'. Mr S turned his back to the view, laid down on his face and plucked grass [*"beside me" in code*]. Then we went on climbing dykes and scrambling over rocks and brushwood to the Loch Roan at the other side of the hill.

O so lovely the Loch was, so calm with dark heather-covered hills at the other side. I put it in my sketch book while luncheon was being got ready, when we ate, and then the gentlemen went shooting. Gertie and I went to meet the carriage as our walk would be too much for her. Mr S, when they met us, preferred going with us to going on shooting with Mr Max, so he did, and one time when he and I were a little behind, we'd a nice wee bit of sensible talk, but I felt a little bit shy of him that day for no reason and did not know what to talk about.

That night Lady Reid, her son and daughter, came to stay till Wednesday. Very nice they all were. Lady Reid talked so nicely to me next morning while I was alone with her in the drawing-room about peace and its cause. I did like it so much and longed to kiss her on the spot, dear old thing. Then I took Mary Reid for a walk to the Glen and talked to her, but though she knew it all perfectly, her heart didn't seem much in it, but then she was very young, poor little thing. Mr S was to have gone away that day, but he asked Gertie if she would mind his staying till the end of the week instead, so she gave him leave. I generally went out every morning to a bridge over a little stream on the way to the gamekeeper's, where there was a clean stone to sit upon, and many a long meditation did I have there, grave and gay, and the stone was a good friend for a confidante, I found.

One morning I went to see Mrs Ferguson, the gardener's wife, who had broken her collar-bone and 2 ribs, and read to her. On Friday there was a dinner-party at Captain Walker's, which Gertie had asked permission to bring Cis and me to, but as Mr S was still there, she couldn't leave him, so Cis caught at the idea of being left at home and eventually the Maxwells, Mr. S. and I went to it. We discussed names going there and had rather an amusing drive, but I didn't enjoy the party much. I was rather interested by my two neighbours at dinner, and it was nice feeling in the middle of all those people that somebody else's mind was raised above it all. I couldn't help giving them a grin across the dinner table on the strength of it. It made me very sad to hear my neighbour talk of fishing as such a great source of happiness in life, as if no greater was known.

Coming home, we couldn't settle how to sit in the carriage, so it ended by Mr S and I being on the front seat, Gertie and Mr M on the back. It was all but dark, and Gertie and Mr M were talking together, so we talked too about different texts, especially Mark VIII.34. and he gave me a long lecture about it, for he thought I put a stronger meaning to it than I really did. Then we spoke of sorrow and its different phases, and he told me about his father's death and what a great sorrow it had been to all of them, but we arrived at home all too soon for my taste, and his too. The Maxwells asked him to stay till Monday, when we were to go to Mossknowe, so he said he would. He and Mr M were out shooting every day so that we never saw anything of them till the evening hardly.

Sunday, our last day, was a very happy one. We drove off early to Dumfries for the English service and H.C. and thoroughly enjoyed it. On the way there we read to ourselves and Mr S showed me his favourites in Ancient and Modern and read me some. We were divided in Church among 2 pews, but it was luxury having our own prayers and being allowed to kneel, and we'd some hymns that we knew and such a delicious sermon on Rev 1. 5 and 6, and then the H.C. so <u>very</u> refreshing, and it was so nice having it just our last day all together, only I did long to be quiet coming home, instead of which we had to talk and come down so soon again to earth. Mr. S. got on the box, so he enjoyed himself in peace.

In the afternoon we went for our Sunday walk but not this time to the Glen, but to a hill overlooking Speddoch. Mr S and I got a little separated from the others and he began saying how quiet and peaceful the day was and that it suited so well with his own feelings, for he had been so very happy since he came, and had enjoyed greater peace there than he had had for a long time. I was very glad to hear this, for it looked as if we had been a little help to him. I was longing to ask him why he had been unhappy then, but I didn't like quite.

Then we joined the others and deposited Cis and her campstool in a wood while we went on. Had to climb two dikes which I wished they would let me get over quite alone, and got into marshes, etc. Somehow we two could not help getting together in front several times, but as the Maxwells constantly called us back for some reason or other, I feared they thought I oughtn't to go so much with him, so stuck to Mr Maxwell's side ever after. I hate the way they nod and beckon and chaff, it makes one uncomfortable when there's no earthly cause, yet they are very good about it too, only they can't resist a little fun. I can't help thinking Mr S likes Llecic Notsmirg [*Cicell Grimston*] so I allow myself a little fun in that direction too. Nous verrons ce que nous verrons. [*I won't insult you, dear reader, by translating this.*] We came back by the glen and sat halfway and sang hymns, the last ones alas, then through the pinery and sat at the seat on the top and sang some more.

The cryptic passage which follows looks as if written in a Scandinavian language.

We asked Mr S for his photo, which he promised us and got ours in return. Asked Cis to copy the Harvest Home for him and was so mournful all the evening, poor man, gazing into the fire for so long. The Maxwells have asked us to go for a week to the Cumberland lakes with them, and asked him too, and he says he will come if only he does not find that his mother wants him at home. It is funny, my journal, isn't it, that he should come up so far again just for a week. What motive can he have? or has he any besides enjoying the thought of the trip.

Monday morning came. Mr Maxwell gathered a lovely bunch of pinks for Cis and me which we treasured up in remembrance of Speddoch and our happy days. Mr Saunders went away at 10 1/2. We went rather later, drove with Gertie into Dumfries, as she wanted to shop, and arrived at Mossknow all right.

Gordon Graham comes on Wednesday. We drove to Gretna on Tuesday and saw the house where the marriages used to be. Cis and Mary went outside, me inside with Mrs Graham. One evening Mary, Cis and I laid on our bed and talked. Mary shewed us the back of the family screen. Why are some people's lives so much happier than others? Life is a curious riddle.

Gordon came and puzzles us very much. He's like Will in some things, hides a great deal under his moustache. Cis and I will soon have to take to "Plenty of hot water" for our spirits have got a bad attack of indigestion.

A very curious letter arrived on Thursday from Gertie which made <u>Cis</u> grow deadly pale and whisper to me, "It depends on me whether he comes or not." We rushed up after breakfast and consulted together over it but found it had not such a defined meaning as we at first supposed, and we think matters still stand much as they were before. We await anxiously a letter from Gertie tomorrow to tell us the meaning of the other letter. How I should like to jump to the other side of next week.

On Sunday we had a very happy day of it. They told us there was a disagreeable clergyman and advised us to take books to Church with us, but instead we liked him very much. He gave us a beautiful sermon on following fully, which hit one very hard. Maybe after all Cis and I will change places in our views of life. How I wish I knew what was right to do.

We had a long walk in the afternoon, leaving Cis half way to read as usual, and a fine scramble we had up a marshy bank above the river, got shoals of blackberries and came back over a fence and a brook which we crossed by the help of a branch and an old tin pail. This was our last day. I'd a nice wee bit of talk with Old Mrs Graham, but we wished we could have spoken to the Colonel and the Captain. Cis talked to Rosa.

On Monday morning we heard from home that Agatha Jennings is dead. Poor thing! How we wish we had spoken to her. Mary and Mr W Sandford went with us as far as Carlisle, where the Maxwells met us and we went on to Penrith, then took to a wagonnet and drove all round Ulswater. O so exquisite with the lights and shadows, my pet shadows, and the mountains! We got one time to see a waterfall, Aira Force, then drove back round Ulswater to Troutbeck to go by train to Keswick. We were in wild spirits and enjoyed our drive thoroughly. Had a nice time to warm ourselves before the train came, and when it did come, out hopped a somebody to whom you have been already introduced, my journal. Many warm greetings ensued, we all hopped into the train again and arrived at Keswick, our destination for the next few days.

And here we are still, and as the others won't go to bed I shall write you. Our first day here Tuesday Oct 16, we all started for Skiddaw with 3 ponies between us.

It was a lovely day and we could see a long way and such beautiful views of Derwentwater. As we went up I resolved to run down before the others and sketch. So nice being on a mountain again, only very *infra dig* riding up. We didn't stay long at the top as it was so freezing, so we retraced our steps and Mr Saunders and I ran on to do my sketch. We had a very nice talk on the way about his London work, and work in general, and the way to work, and what to say and how to say it and about forgiveness and the right life and the hidden life and people and not being ashamed to speak and when not to speak, etc., etc. Then when the others came down I hadn't quite done my sketch, so we stayed on and talked of plans and Ventnor and possibility of seeing people again, etc. And so we came home again in very good spirit, quite ready for luncheon. I was much amused at being able to read Mr M's thoughts in his face; destined to be disappointed.

After luncheon we all went down to the lake and went out boating. O so luxurious with the plash of the oars in the still, mirror-like water and the lovely blue misty hills, and we sang hymns as we went along, which seemed to hallow it all so nicely.

We got out once to see Borrowdale Force, not much in the way of a waterfall, but we got some remembrance bits from it. I found a lilac flower to go side by side with a shamrock leaf which was given me. Then we took to our boat again and got a lot of reeds, which we splashed each other with and finally stuck in our hats, and O the sunset as we went home again, tingeing all the water, and the moon came from the other side and embossed it in silver. I could have stayed out for ever, but we were obliged to go in as it was getting chilly.

As we went home, Cis, and I and Mr S. had a race, he hopping, we running and in fits of laughter at his appearance, for he had got a railway rug like a shawl round him and looked exactly like a crow who had been shot in the leg and was hopping away wounded with a pointed tail. People must have thought us rather mad going through the town, I suspect. In the evening we adjourned to a lower drawing-room and sang. Somebody seemed to take a great interest in my singing!

Next morning we all went to be photographed, and were done twice in groups, but one was bad. Each time I noticed that Mr S. put himself next to me, and commented upon it in my own mind. Then we got into a waggonet and took a long drive and a lovely one. Went to see the Lodore Falls, but were very disappointed in them. I put Cis in purgatory by making her stand on a rickety bridge and then dancing the perfect care [?] upon it. Then on we went till we came to the Bowder Stone, a gigantic stone tumbled from the mountain, when we bundled out again and climbed to the top.

Mr S. went more with Cis today, and I tried to be very glad. Soon after, the two gentlemen and I turned out to walk up a steep hill, but I soon got tired and had to go slow and rest awhile, and Mr S. waited for me and got me mosses while I sat down. Rather nice of him, thought I.

Next we came to Honister Crag, so wild and stern and rugged. We had to go down worse hills than I have ever gone down in my life, but this time I didn't walk. We called to a miner to show us how they slid down the slate from the quarry, so he came down a most awful place with a slate cart behind him (O what a mess I've made!) [*Octavia had managed to smudge the ink on the last sentence.*]

Then we drove on to Buttermere. Perfectly beautiful it was, though very wild, and we had luncheon on char at an inn and inspected all the poetical rubbish that visitors had left in the book, then drove home again well tired and slept a good deal in the evening.

My journal, it's an odd fact that Mr S. always puts himself next to me at meals, which he needn't do the least unless he liked. Nonsense, child! Don't talk rubbish. I'm sure he never thinks about it a bit.

The next day we settled to drive to Ambleside for one night, taking the Druid Stones [*Castlerigg Stone Circle, I assume*] on the way. We got out to see them and had to climb a very high stile to get into the field where they were. I, being of an independent nature, preferred jumping from the top by myself to taking anybody's hand to help me. The consequence was....

How ashamed I was of myself, and was obliged for the rest of the day to become a longer and thinner girl.

It rained nearly all the way, however we managed to sing a little in the carriage to beguile the way, and the weather kindly clearing when we got to Ambleside we sallied forth to see Stock Ghyll Force. The others would run on and leave me with Mr S, which I didn't like, so begged Cis to stick by me. Poor man, he tumbled over a stone and cut his knee very badly one time. We liked this fall very much; it was full of water after the rain.

Our little parlour had a piano in it, so I played all my ------ things and sang a bit, and somebody seemed to enjoy it very much. We took a long muddy walk to see the Windermere lake about 2 miles off, but I didn't enjoy it for I was tired, and minus crinoline, and felt stupid and afraid of Cis tiring herself, etc.

Next morning (Friday) off we set again in a waggonet and drove 43 miles to Furness to see the abbey there, only stopping once for an hour at Coniston to rest the horses, during which time we all walked off to see Dungeon Ghyll Force.

Mr Maxwell had given Cis a bit of holly for her hat, and on me remarking I'd like us all to have a bit, Mr S ran and pricked his fingers severely in attempting to get some, but it had no berries, so when they came to a tree with berries Mr Max and Mr S got a lot more and somebody ran up to me saying, "I was so afraid Mr Maxwell would forestall me and prevent my having the pleasure of giving you some." He got us many bits more, and ferns as remembrances, and remarked that a certain leaf was the shape of a perfect heart.

We had a good climb up to the Fall which was very pretty, between two dark rocks and stones and ferns like a dungeon, and talked pleasantly the while. Then coming down again we returned to our waggonet and continued our journey, but Mr S. seemed very unwilling to turn out and walk up the hills, on which Cis hinted that he was lazy, which seemed to hurt his feelings, and he begged to remark it was not laziness which made him loath to turn out, so amused himself in his walk gathering some heather, which he gave to me.

We passed through the loveliest scenery. Soft, tree-covered hills in front and grassy slopes and tarns and rivers with the huge and grand Langdale Pikes lowering above, having their ruggedness relieved by a streak of soft sunlight falling on them, and in the further distance soft blue mountains lost in the clouds. O it was exquisite.

Bye and bye we came to softer scenery which verged into comparative flatness, and so we arrived at Furness. Had much amusement from conversing with a small boy who clung on to the carriage. A charming hotel was the Station one, and such nice rooms which the old nurse had engaged for us, she having come a shorter way by coach. We were tired with our drive, so took it easy in the evening, and my creature comforts were well attended to, not by myself.

Not having a piano to amuse us, we took an insane desire to see the abbey by moonlight at half past ten. No sooner said than done, and we all sallied forth as it was a deliciously warm night and the abbey was quite close. And O it was so pretty, though there was not much moon, but the dim arches looked so grand and black against the sky, and the darkness and silence but a mystery to it all.

A beautiful Abbey it seemed to be, and we only longed for the daylight to see it more thoroughly, and next morning, the light having come, we once more went to inspect it and poked into every nook and corner, and Mr S got clematis and ivy and ferns as mementos from the wall. A grand old Abbey it must have been, and a grand old ruin it is now.

So, having inspected it thoroughly, we went for a walk up a hill, which I didn't care to do as I was very tired, but thought it would seem stupid not to go, but somehow I longed for a good cry and felt oppressed as I used to at Speddoch.

What goes up must come down, which we found to be once more true, and having found a place where the Abbey looked its best, I asked Mr S for my sketchbook, which he generally carried for me in his pocket, and sat down to sketch. He sat down too behind me and began to talk. Talked about its being nearly our last day together and bewailed its being so, which I joined in. Then he said, "Well! I trust that if we never meet again on earth, we may in Heaven," and said he blessed the day on which he had first met us at Speddoch, but said it was such a chance his ever meeting us again, on which I remarked I didn't look upon it as such an impossibility, and should be sorry to do so as we knew each other so well, now, and had all been so happy together. "Well but", says he, "I don't know how I could manage it, for I could hardly come and call upon Mrs Grimston, she would think it so odd." "Would she?" says I, "I don't know much about etiquette in those matters, but I don't think she would mind, for she knows you quite well from hearsay." "Does she?" says he, seeming much comforted. "Well, shall I ask Mrs Maxwell what she thinks?" "Do," said I. "She would know best about it."

Then we had some good talk, and he asked me to pray for him, which I said I would, and asked him to do the same for me, on which he said, "I do already, and shall do so to the end of my life." Then we walked down together to the hotel, as we didn't see the others and I had done my sketch, and coming downstairs from seeing after my packing I found him on the sofa in a deep study.

The others soon came in and we had luncheon, after which we went to the train and went by it a bit and then by carriage as far as Windermere, Newby Bridge, to catch the steamer for Low Wood. In the carriage, Mr Maxwell would talk about what a pity it was that young ladies mightn't write to young gentlemen, etc., etc.

In the steamer we were arranged thus...

...and presently I heard Mr S and Gertie beginning a very earnest conversation. Guessing the subject, I carefully turned my back to Gertie and admired the prospect the other way, but caught a few words spoken louder than the rest which turned my guesses into certainty.

I tried to talk to the nurse and play with the baby to take off the old lady's attention from her opposite neighbours, and presently the voices ceased and Mr S walked off to the other end of the steamer. I turned to Gertie and said, "Does he care for me?" "Yes," said Gertie. My heart jumped nearly into my mouth, and I can't say the feeling was comfortable.

The lake, the hills, the sunset, everything seemed completely to have changed their colour. I would fain have sunk through the steamer into the lake, but it could not be, and there I was in for it and must face it. Oh, it was dreadful, and now the others would go off to the other end of the boat where Mr S. was, and I had to talk as if I knew nothing about it.

Bye and bye we arrived at our destination, Low Wood, and Mr S would put on my cloak and carry my umbrella. The Hotel was close to the landing place, but I felt quite a different person from when I had left *terra firma* an hour before. Having settled what rooms to have, we sallied forth for a walk. I longed to stay at home and have time to think a little, but thought it would look odd, so went too, but stuck close to Gertie all the way.

When we had gone far enough and were turning back, Cis dawdled behind over some ferns, and said to Mr S, "I want to speak to you for a minute." "Do you?" said he. "Yes," said Cis, "I want to speak to you about what Gertie and you were talking of in the steamer. Is it true that you care for Octavia?" "Yes," said he, and then they had a long talk which I was longing to know the purport of, but walked on goodly in front and took no notice.

It was dark when we came in, and he said, "I think I shall go upstairs straight to dress." "Do," says Cis. "I think you had much better." Then Cis went to Gertie's room, where was also Mr M, and the three had a grand consultation, while I went upstairs to be quiet a bit, and soon Cis came up and told me all about it. The first thing I did was to throw myself on the bed and kick up my heels in the air. He asked her if there was any chance for him. Her answer being favourable, he asked her when she thought it would be best. She said the sooner the better. Would Monday do before we part? Why not Sunday? The better day, the better deed. So it was settled for Sunday at the first opportunity.

I hated so coming down that evening, but it had to be gone through, and he sat beside me and somehow it got over and I sang a great deal, while somebody buried their face in their hands on the sofa, and thus passed Saturday night before the dreadful eventful Sunday. That night I had one nightmare after another, first of proposals, then of weddings and was awake long before it was time to get up in the morning. Cis was perfectly cracked and out of her wits with glee, while I shivered in my shoes.

It looked dull and cloudy, though Cis declared it was going to clear and be a beautiful day. We settled to drive to

Church at Ambleside and walk back. At the mention of "walk back" my heart visited my boots, but however we did drive there and Mr Maxwell, Mr Saunders and I got in about the third pew from the top at the right hand side of the Church, while Gertie and Cis got in the middle aisle somewhere.

It was desperate work trying to control one's thoughts till the sermon, and then... Never did I hear such a sermon before, and never do I expect to again. It was on Prov III 5, "In all thy ways acknowledge Him and He shall direct thy path." And if it had been written for us all it couldn't have been better. It said we need never to fear about anything if it had been well prayed over, but to commit our way to the Lord and He would bring it to pass, and much more which I cannot remember, but which I hope was not therefore lost. Coming out of Church, Cis gave his hand such a hearty squeeze, which he returned with a blessing and tears in his eyes.

This service seemed quite to hallow what we all knew was going to happen: it all seemed so guided. We walked to the hotel and had luncheon, then set out for a walk. Went as far as the church all together, but the opening of the churchyard gate brought me and him in front of the others, who instantly began to dawdle behind. I turned round and gave Gertie a despairing glance, and now we were fairly launched, and happening to turn my eyes round once again I spied the others disappearing round the other corner of the church.

Well, now I couldn't help myself, so it was as well to make the best of it. We went round the back of the Church to a little lych-gate which no sooner had we passed through than he turned round to me and with a tremble in his voice said, "Miss Octavia, beneath the shadow of this church I wish to speak to you about something which you perhaps have heard about and know what I am going to say." "I do," said I. - He went on: "Mrs M. and Cicell both gave me some hope, will you also tell me if there is any chance of your ever caring for me?" "I will indeed," said I. "God bless you for that," he said, taking my hand. [*Following the section I have deciphered, there is a cryptic sentence which is beyond me.*]

I cannot remember what more passed between us, but I followed C's directions implicitly about ----- ------ and by this time our walk had extended through a delicious shrubbery-like walk till we got to the gate leading to Fox Howe, over which we leaned and talked till we thought it must be time to be going homewards, so back we turned and soon found the others waiting for us on a seat. I gave Cis a wink and grin, at which Gertie ran up and embraced me with many congratulations, while Mr M shook hands with Herbert, who was so completely overcome with joy that <u>he kissed Cis and Gertie</u> and finally succumbed on the seat for a few minutes, after which he and I went on in front and the others followed, after having a private embrace among themselves for joy at the affair. Herbert gave me his Mount of Olives to read some time, then we all went and sat in the church porch and were just beginning to sing a hymn when the bells set up a regular peal and clashed just as if for a wedding. It sounded so jolly and seemed like a sort of good omen coming just then. We went into church and sat in the same pew as before for the service, which we enjoyed very much tho' the sermon was nothing much in any way.

After it we walked home, and I secured a little quiet time before dinner at which we were treated to Champagne and had our healths drunk, etc., etc. Plenty of singing went on in the evening, and very happy were we all. Then Gertie proposed a walk in the garden, so putting on our cloaks, out we went. It was a lovely moonlight night, and we paraded for some time, but I got greatly laughed at afterwards for being so shy of Herbert, not daring to take his arm or anything, so settled not to be so stupid and shy next time.

This aforesaid "next time" happened to be in the train next morning, leaving the Lakes, and so happening to put my hand on the partition between me and Herbert it was instantly seized on, which Gertie gave a wink and smile of approbation.

We soon had all to part, Cis and I to go to Murraythwaite, Gertie and Mr Maxwell to Southwick and Herbert to London. Kendall Junction was the parting place, and our spirits were not of the highest at the thought Herbert was to go to Kilnwick 'on approval' in a few days, which he did, and took all their hearts by storm. So Mama signified her consent, fully and freely giving, and we were engaged, on the strength of which we began writing to each other.

Our Murraythwaite visit was a very pleasant one, but we missed the Maxwells and Herbert very much and longed to go home. The Murray girls were there, and Captain Graham and Mary came for a few days, so we had a nice time of it and Gracie herself was charming, but we felt we had had enough excitement and wanted rest. "So the day it came at last" when we left again the hospitable homes of Scotland filled with pleasant memories and turned homewards.

By the time we got near Hull, I began to be a little anxious and excited, but my anxiety was rewarded by seeing Jin, Maudie and Herbert on the platform waiting for us. Nothing much happened till we got in the train to Lockington, and then Herbert said, "I declare I am not going to wait any longer, but think this quite private enough to have my first kiss!" So saying, I felt myself surrounded by two long arms and a hearty one he had and Jin looked north, Maudie south, Cis east, but could not succeed in shutting their ears so effectually as they had done their eyes, so recommended us to put up an umbrella next time to shut out both sight and sound. We came home in the Bus, a tiring end to a tiring day, and were not sorry to reach home, where Monk and Buttons [*dogs?*] received us with many grins.

So the next few days passed, my first experience of engaged life, but I cannot say I thought it the Elysium that one reads of. I never know what I might or might not do, and could not help a certain constraint which was not conducive to perfect happiness. We used to sit in the library and write letters all the morning, and sometimes go out and read on the seat in the shrubbery. Mama asked Arthur to come to Kilnwick, as he was soon going out to Canada and otherwise would not see me, so one day when we were at 5 o'clock tea, engaged in unpacking a travelling bag which had just come from Walter, and with all our hands in the bag pulling out one thing after another amid roars of laughter, in walked the said Arthur.

He was not a bit like Herbert in personal appearance, and looked much amused at our employment. He stayed 3 days and then Herbert and he went back to Town together. About this time settlement bothers began, and great bothers they were, everybody misunderstanding everybody, and my daily letters to Herbert had to do their little utmost to comfort and make up for the bothers. [*In those days you had to pay someone to take a daughter off your hands.*]

On Nov 20 Maudie, Cis and I went up to Town to stay with my future mother-in-law. It was formidable work and I dreaded it much. We took Maudie with us a bit of the way on her way to Leamington, but got the wrong tickets at Hull and had to go by another line, so missing Herbert who had gone off to Bedford to meet us.

Arthur ,however, came to meet us and so we arrived at Bolton Gardens and were met in the hall by Mrs Saunders and Eliza. I instantly lost my heart to the former, she was so nice to me, and Eliza I liked very much too. Herbert didn't turn up till we were just going to dinner, so they left us upstairs to greet each other and I enjoyed my stay in London very much, spent all my days trousseau-getting and saw Herbert in the evening.

We went home again on the 30th and Cis went to join Maudie at Leamington. I became very business-like, had such lots to do in the way of trousseau, and such loads of congratulatory letters to answer. Herbert came up again to Kilnwick on Dec. 11 and stayed till the 18th, which was the last I saw of him before he came up for our wedding on Jan 7.

We had a very sober Xmas, though the Willies came to help us to enjoy it. A few days after, the Trenches came to stay with us, Charley, Myrie and Lizzie. We had asked Thomas, but Charley came instead. We had hard work to amuse them till the wedding week, as there was deep snow which put a stop to shooting or anything pleasant for Charley and he got a little bored.

O how I longed to be quiet and alone during the short time that was left of my unmarried life, but perhaps it was better for me not to be, for I had to stir myself up to the utmost to amuse them all and that kept me from brooding over leaving home to be launched on the unknown future. In one of our gambols one wet day, I sprained my ankle which kept me a prisoner to the sofa for some days, but the Trenches took great care of me, and I got quite fond of Charley as he was so very kind to me.

So passed away 1866. I sat up to see the end of it, and I knew Herbert was doing the same, and I sat and thought over my fire a great deal; indeed over my fire was the only time I had to think, so I hardly ever got to bed before 1 or 2 in the morning. I was not able to bid any of the villagers goodbye before I was married, because of my ankle, which entirely prevented my walking and which was a great disappointment to me.

And now I come to my wedding, which deserves to be in a separate story to itself, so I must close this, which has trespassed already beyond its proper bounds as its name "A Peep into Scotland" will show.

Part Five
My Wedding
Beginning from the Sunday before, Jan 6. 1867

My last Sunday at home. The ground covered with snow and so cold. It was the turn for two services, morning and evening, but somehow I couldn't enjoy my services much. The thought of the harmonium playing, and its being my last Sunday, disturbed me. Mr Jennings preached very nicely on the beginning of a new year and new periods of our life. As I was playing the voluntary he came up to me, and when I had done shook hands with me, saying, "You must allow me to repeat on your behalf the blessing which I have just pronounced." Then he bid me goodbye with such a kind smile, dear old soul.

I did like him so much for saying that to me; it helped to cheer up my Sunday very much, though I could not resist one good howl. Then I had my last teaching of my boys. Little by little, as the minutes went by, I felt my roots being pulled up like a tree going to be transplanted.

Charlie amused himself by building a snow-man for my benefit while I was at school. Then came evening service. I couldn't help dawdling over my concluding voluntary which was my farewell to the harmonium, in fact wished very much to put a drag on the wings of old Time, not having trust enough in my composition to enter upon a new phase of my life without compunction.

On Monday we had plenty to do, preparing for the people who were coming, and about 6pm Maudie, Cis and Herbert appeared. We had a grand unpacking of presents in the evening, in the middle of which Mary Graham walked in. We had not heard the carriage, so did not go to meet her or anything, poor thing.

On Tuesday Eliza, the Stopfords and Captain Nicholson, the best man, arrived.

Wednesday. Walter came and I packed all day and we had many games in the evening. Captain Nicholson was very amusing, and we liked him very much. Herbert slept at Mrs Nicholson's that night.

How I did dawdle over my fire and think, and all night I did not sleep much more than half an hour. The snow had all melted, leaving everything in a dreadfully wet state, and that night there was a most awful storm of hail and rain and wind all the time, to which I listened and thought of the morrow.

O those weary hours as one by one they passed, and at last a gray drizzling morning dawned. I did not go down to breakfast, but had mine in my room and held a levee of all my bridesmaids. So nice they all looked in white grenadine with blue rosettes at intervals round the bottom and blue silk peplums and blue crepe bonnets with white dewy pompon roses and Cluny lace and pearls. At 10 I dressed in bridal costume, namely white ribbed silk trimmed with satin and fringes and an enormously long train, white tulle veil spotted with chenille and wreath with two long trails of flowers hanging down.

I first studied the marriage service, then I went and had a good warm at the breakfast-room fire, and listened to all the carriages driving off to the Church one after another, feeling that it was all for poor little me, and feeling mighty small in consequence. Presently Walter rushed in saying, "Come along! The carriage is here!" and off I went to the carriage, quite forgetting the lovely bridal bouquet which Herbert had brought for me. We went through the shrubbery and walked up to the church from the gate. There was a great crowd of people round the church door and all my bridesmaids waiting in the porch. Crowds inside the church too. As we came into church little Bartle began his voluntary on the harmonium, but I didn't hear it, for everything seemed to pass before my eyes as in a dream. I just saw Herbert on the altar steps, but none of the fine decorations which were put up in my honour.

So we were married, Alex doing the chief part of the service and the Dean of Peterborough the remainder. It all seemed so very soon over. And now my old name was signed for the last time and we drove home where I was kissed all round and longed to run away. Next came the breakfast. Herbert made two very neat little speeches, and there were cheers, etc, after which, and having cut the wedding cake, I went up to get ready, and being late had to bundle anyhow into my things and had hardly time to take a last look at my room.

There was happily no time for a scene, and off we went among the usual shower of old shoes and cheers in the britska, open with the head up and 4 grey horses who went at a gallop up the approach. The wedding party and bridesmaids did look so pretty outside the hall door as we drove off in the sun, for by this time the day was bright and beautiful and the bells were ringing so nicely as I left my home forever, for now it is but my secondary home. There was a crowd of farmers outside Nicholsons as we passed, and who gave us a cheer.

ARTHUR C. VENTRESS

Part Six

My Honeymoon in France & Italy

We were in plenty of time for the train, where on the way to Hull I gave Herbert my first real kiss. At Hull we went to the refreshment room and wrote to the two mothers, till it was time for the Matlock train, and arrived at Matlock about 8 o'clock, very tired after the exiting day. It seemed so strange sitting opposite Herbert at dinner alone, after which I sang to him, as there was a piano in the room, till about half pat ten, when Herbert, suggesting that I must be tired, I said I would see if Gibbons [*Elizabeth Gibbons, a lady's maid in the household of Herbert's mother*] had unpacked for me, and finding she had, did not appear again.

Next morning, after writing some letters, we went to explore the town and all its marble shops, which were very tempting, and bought a little thing for Captain Nicholson as a reward for acting as best man.

The afternoon found us driving to Haddon Hall, a delicious old place with a ghost-like Terrace and broad steps up to it, and a long line of time-worn yew trees throwing a dark shadow all down the Terrace, and making one think how it must look at night with fitful gleams of moonshine coming through the interlaced boughs, and a melancholy owl or two screeching round the old towers.

There was a large, or rather long and narrow ballroom opening through an antechamber on to the said Terrace, and we amused ourselves having a walk all down it, while our guide looked stolidly on at our gambols. We liked the old place very much, and enjoyed our day.

The next morning found us on our way to Canterbury. We stopped half an hour in London, where mother met us with a hamper of nice things to take with us. Our Sunday was nice and quiet, a true rest-day after the week's toil and excitement. We went to the cathedral and had the Communion for the first time together as man and wife. It seemed like a true beginning of our married life.

Monday we crossed from Folkestone, meeting an old aunt of Herbert's at the station. On the steamer, calmly pacing up and down, was Mr Marshall of Patrington, whom I did not care particularly to meet at that time, so appeared utterly unconscious of his presence. We got to Paris that night and while at dinner in the Restaurant of the Grande Hotel, who should appear again but Mr Marshall, who sat down at the table next to us. The same thing happened the next morning and I began to feel a terrible sense of rudeness in thus cutting him dead, but now that I had done it so long, I was ashamed to recognise him at last.

We went sightseeing a good deal to the Maison Cluny, Louvre, Palais Royal, Bois de Boulogne, etc, but were much disappointed by not seeing the Emperor in the Bois. After a few days in Paris we went to Lyons for one night, then to Marseilles, where who should turn up to haunt us like a bad shilling but Mr Marshall who was found calmly eating his dinner in the hotel when we came to ours. We met him once again, nay twice, at breakfast, and in the Town, when he vanished and has been seen no more from that time to this.

Marseilles was not the least the dirty, narrow-streeted town that I expected, but in a drive that we took to see the place it seemed to me to have plenty of broad streets and handsome houses in them, and one of the loveliest views from the road above the sea. In front the Mediterranean, which bye the bye ought to have been blue but wasn't, in a silver-gray dress lighted up with streaks of brilliants beyond which were hazy blue mountains losing themselves mysteriously in cloud and sea. Turning round one saw promontories and islands and the Chateaux d'If on its lonely rock, and bits of the town appearing from among olive trees, and white houses with their red roofs among cypresses and broom. It was very lovely, and the young couple who might have been seen that morning in a carriage driving along by the sea, and contemplating the beauties here described, were superlatively happy. I may here remark that the snow which had followed us hitherto, and in some places was some feet deep, now disappeared and gave place to the brightest and sunniest weather which shone upon us for the rest of our honeymoon.

It was the 19th when we got to Nice, and truly nice it was to see orange trees and olives for the first time in my life, and to come to perfect summer. We went to the Hotel Chauvain and found that kind hands had put there the loveliest of bridal bouquets to greet our arrival - real orange blossom and myrtle, etc, smelling so delicious.

We soon adjourned to the Rue Gioffredo, found the Dukes and Bess had just done dinner, and much warm greeting ensued, and many things had we to say to each other. I was given a lovely locket from Duke and Flo and an opal ring from Bess.

We stayed 10 days at Nice, during that time seeing a great deal of Gioffredo party besides Ed Saunderson and Helena, to whom I took a great fancy, and making one or two expeditions; one to Villefranche, such a pretty place all among olives and scarlet geranium growing wild. We had a picnic down by the sea and enjoyed ourselves much.

After we left the Chauvain, we heard that an old maid inhabited the room next to ours and heard all we said to each other, detailing the same, much spiced, to the diners at the table d'hote. She said Herbert called me his "princess" and "golden-haired angel" and after saying sweet things to each other we read selections out of the bible together.

We made a nice little plan to carry off Bess with us on our further tour to Geuda, which after many scruples of conscience about joining people on their honeymoon, she agreed to, and we started in high spirits.

By the way, we made one delightful expedition from Nice to St Audré, a lovely valley which abounded in maidenhair growing most luxuriantly all over the banks, and great ---- locks hung above at each side lit up with wee bits of sunshine and many colours. I sketched the castles and we voted that one of our happiest days. Driving there we heard someone passing say "Come bella" which delighted Herbert and has been a great joke ever since.

Well, to resume, Bess, Herbert and I started in a carriage on one of the most glorious days ever known, in which everything in nature seemed to agree. We wound up a very high hill from which a most exquisite view of Nice was to be seen, and the deep blue sea, for it really was blue this time, till suddenly we turned round a corner and in front of us was a grand range of mountains topped with snow and golden light. We stopped for me to sketch it, then continued our way, coming again to the sea, the road winding in and out above it, had our luncheon on some rocks just over Monaco, the great gambling place.

Then we went on again to Mentone where we stopped for the night. I longed to stop longer there, it was so pretty, but we tried to see as much as we could of the place before returning our ----- [*carriage?*] next morning. We rather shocked Bessie by the way we behaved on the road, not being so afraid of people's opinion or so fond of propriety as that young person, but we were very happy, and what more did we want? We came across Lady Crewe and her daughters at the table d'hote and spent the evening with them afterwards, I being afflicted with a bad attack of hay asthma the while, which slightly spoilt my pleasures.

Once more away, sometimes with 3, sometimes 4

horses, galloping downhill, walking up, enlivened by the coachman's peculiar way of cheering the horses, much resembling sounds often heard at sea.

Lunched at Turbia [*Italy*] on paté de foie gras and cherry brandy. Reached Oneglia well tired and ready for bed. I had the prettiest little bed surrounded by mosquito-curtains, not that any of the dreaded tribe ever came near us.

Once more on again, the road this time going more inland and giving us lovely peeps at the Maritime Alps and on the other side aloes and reeds, then the dark blue sea which this time made even the dark blue sky look faded. We passed through delightful old villages, though not in every way pleasing to the senses, and the female part of the inhabitants seemed to consist in old hags or children, some very handsome ones, but we were mostly disappointed in the beauty of the people.

Stopped half way for a few hours at San Remo, where after refreshing ourselves we sallied forth to see whatever was to be seen. Took up our abode on a kind of pier and proceeded to sketch, on which we were immediately surrounded by about 30 men and women all jabbering Italian and making jokes at our expense, some dancing about in front of us, putting themselves in graceful attitudes for us to draw. Bess tried her hand at Italian, which amused them much, and our sketchbooks were handed round when we had finished for them to see themselves depicted, and their exclamations of delight and horror combined, as the frights we made of them were too absurd.

San Remo was a most quaint old town; we wished we could have seen more of it, but 2 hours was all the time we had to give it. Savona was our resting place for the night, but as we got there very late and left very early, having a long day before us, we saw nothing of it hardly.

We had many long steep hills to climb between Savona and Genoa, so used to get out and walk up them and get flowers, and sometimes Herbert would walk on quite far and then hide behind rocks and throw things at us or jump out upon us as we passed.

When we stopped to bait, we walked up to a place belonging to a Count Pallavicino, where were the most wonderful gardens. Our showman could only speak Italian, so not very much conversation passed between us. There was one place in the garden, an arbour of roses where we turned a tap and all the roses dropped water upon us and little fountains sprung up in all directions. Then he took us to a swing, into which I got, when suddenly a fountain sprung up beneath me giving me a shower every time I passed through it. This Gibbons was delighted at, who was sitting a little way off, on which the man said, "We will give a little to the lady who laughed," and forthwith came a little fountain straight at her.

After this little amusement, we went to see a grotto of real stalactites, brought from a distance, so pretty as it was, with a little lake running into it on which we went on a boat. We were finally given some camellias, which were growing on large shrub-like bushes in the open-air, then started again for Genoa, well pleased with what we had seen.

Our first sight of Genoa was enchanting. It was on suddenly turning a corner of the road, and the sun was just setting, making the hills of a rich purple. It was so lovely, and the town, too, delighted us as we passed through it to the Hotel Royale, where we took up our abode for a week. It was a curious fact that at the table d'hôte nothing but English was to be heard spoken, though there were a good many people there.

We had nice rooms looking onto the harbour and the sea, and in the evening it was so hot we all leaned out of the windows and listened to whatever sounds Genoa produced, which consisted of a distant sound of the sea, a plash of oars and ripple in the harbour, a little breeze whispering among the forest of masts, occasionally a clatter of sabots and a few words in Italian, or a snatch of a song. Once or twice we heard some men coming along singing a chorus in parts, as only Italians can sing, and so pretty as it sounded in the still night air.

Thursday we arrived, and on Friday we prepared for sightseeing. We therefore took a carriage and went to deliver our letter of introduction to the English clergyman, hoping to hear from him what we should go and see. He, however, was out, so we had to follow our own devices, which led us to see the different churches, and most beautiful they were. All the pillars of different coloured marbles; altar-rails, pavement, everything of marble, and the pictures were most beautiful, many of them, so different from the Romanist Churches in France. There was a great deal of gilding, which looked very handsome.

One time, as Herbert was coming down some marble steps from one of the altars, he slipped and fell on his back, hurting himself very much; on which he was instantly surrounded by several priests jabbering all at once and suggesting various remedies, the only one of which we could understand being Aqua d'Arnica, whose effect the old priest signified by pretending to be much hurt and rubbing himself violently. I believe Bess thought me very unfeeling, but I could hardly do anything but laugh at the absurdity of the scene, the way the priests jumped up from their prayers and rushed to the scene of action. We made the best use we could of our small stock of Italian to thank them and departed amid a chorus of "Aqua d'Arnica; Aqua d'Arnica," carrying off our wounded hero. We next went to see the Palazzo Rossi and were charmed with the pictures. We quite longed to spend a fortune in buying them. Guido Reni's I admired particularly. The expressions of all his faces were so beautiful.

Then the profusion of white marble delighted us in all the Palaces; broad white marble steps and columns, every place seemed built of marble, and the statues seemed also to abound. We saw many palaces during our stay at Genoa: Palazzos Balbi, Rossi, Doria, Reale and others whose names I forget which were all more or less on the same plan, some with an inner court of white marble arches and pillars with marble chessboard pavement, filled with orange-trees and beautiful plants and all containing lovely pictures.

We next explored the town, which was well worth seeing. The streets were mostly very narrow with hardly any pavement, and the houses very high and rather leaning towards each other, making the sky look quite a narrow strip between them. Herbert said the town reminded him very much of Alexandria, and certainly it was very like what one imagines the towns in the east to be. The bright colours and picturesque figures, and in fact the *tout ensemble,* made one wish one were an artist. We met several girls in Genoese veils made of plain white muslin, and very becoming they were, so much so that Herbert made me promise to get one for myself, but bye the bye I have never done it yet.

Then we went and ruined ourselves among the filigree shops, Bess giving me a very pretty butterfly for my hair to redeem a lost "Bonjour Phillipine". We also bought a few things for our snow-clad relations at home. The principal street was full of nothing but these filigree shops, being the chief things at Genoa, and after ruining ourselves sufficiently among them we happened to go into a book shop, when I instantly fell in love with two pictures hanging up, which Herbert made me a present of. They looked just like oil paintings, but were most wonderfully cheap and we were delighted with our purchase.

At the table d'hote we made acquaintance with Mr and Mrs Elrington, a clergyman and his wife, who made us quite savage by abusing Genoa and saying it was nothing compared to San Remo where they had been. Mrs E. tried to find out everything about us, and our great delight was to avoid her questions. I think Bess being with us puzzled her very much, and I doubt whether she ever discovered we were a bride and bridegroom on our honeymoon tour. There was also a nice old Colonel Vaughan, who had come to nurse a sick son and who invited us to visit him in Shropshire if ever we should be in his neighbourhood.

On Sunday we went to the English church and had a pleasant service, and after it we talked to the clergyman who told us of things yet to be seen, and went with us to see a very curious old Church. He also told us a good deal about the Reformation going on in Italy, and showed us a place where the reformed priests meet at night in secret for fear of persecution for prayer together. He told us we ought to see the promenade, so thither we went and watched the people promenading in all their finery, or sitting at little tables under the trees, drinking lemonade or having ices and criticising their neighbours. There was a glorious view on all sides from the Promenade of snowy mountains and sea and town, which we saw to perfection as it was a glorious day.

About this time a sad reality dawned on our minds i.e. that we must leave this Elysium of sunshine, warmth and beauty and return once more to our fatherland, and the more real business of life. It was an unpleasant thought, for we were so happy, but at last the dreaded time arrived and we departed by night in a steamer to go by sea to Nice, turning our backs most unwillingly upon Italy. It was a cold, stormy night, but nevertheless Herbert and I paced the deck arm in arm for a long time, watching the lights of Genoa grow fainter in the distance and looking at the phosphorous lights in the sea.

While we were thus engaged on deck, my brush and back-hair glass were making a plot below stairs how they should manage to go back to Genoa, they being as unwilling as we were to leave Italian ground. They accomplished their plot by hiding themselves among the bedclothes in the morning, being forgotten, and going back with the steamer next morning. The foolish glass, however, broke his back in his attempt to escape, and has been a cripple ever since, for both he and his companion were finally captured and brought in triumph to Nice.

At Nice we delivered our faithful Bessie back to her friends' care, and after spending a few hours with them we departed for Marseilles, on the way there seeing the most splendid sunset I ever remember. There was a girl in our carriage who was weeping buckets full of tears the whole day long. I made out a history for her that she was going into a convent rather against her will, and had just bid a final adieu to her family.

After sleeping at Marseilles that night we went on to Arles, as we heard there were many things there worth seeing. Providing ourselves with a guide, we sallied forth to see first the museum where there were wonderful old tombs belonging to the old Christians, then to the theatre, a charming old ruined place built by the Romans; next to the Champs Elysees, consisting of a road with rows of old coffins on each side, some Roman, some early Christian, leading to an old chapel where we saw in a coffin the skeleton of a Roman girl, dug up 2 years before, found dressed as a bride and quite entire. All but the skeleton crumbled away, however, on being exposed to the air.

Our guide talked such provincial French that Herbert couldn't understand a word, and I very little, which was rather unsatisfactory. We were also taken to see the Cathedral, which boasted of some beautiful old cloisters attached to it, and we bought a photo of them. Then to the Roman Amphitheatre where we pictured to ourselves the martyrdoms that had happened there in the centuries gone by. It was a beautiful old place, and what I liked best of all about it was my being taken to see the cells where the Christian Martyrs were kept before being brought out to the wild beasts. We came out by the same passage that they always came out by, and for the time being I fancied myself a martyr and tried to feel what they felt.

Our last piece of sightseeing, however, was the most weird of all. It was a catacomb, and we went down some dark narrow steps, with one torch to guide us, till we found ourselves in a good-sized vaulted space strewn with Roman urns, and with dark mysterious-looking nooks and corners in it smelling of the dust of ages. From thence we groped our way along a curious irregular passage, where sometimes we had to stoop it was so low, and by the dim light thrown on our path we could see bones strewn about, human bones, and urns of every kind seeming as if we were walking in the land of departed spirits and making us feel as if we might come in a short time to the river Styx and Charon with his boat waiting to ferry us over. Instead of this, however, we came at last to a large heap of human bones piled up, which our guide touched with his foot to show them to us, and sent several skulls and bones of all kinds rolling to our feet with a strange rattling sound.

I was sorry for the poor old Romans not being allowed to rest their bones in peace, but notwithstanding my pity we singled out one of the best skulls we could find from among his fellows and carried him off as a trophy. I was however eventually more sorry for myself than for him, for Herbert declared I must carry it in my box, which I was obliged to do after wrapping him up in a pocket-handkerchief shroud, and we possess him still as a living, or dead, memorial of our visit to Arles.

Having inspected that town we adjourned to Avignon, where we passed the night and did the palace of the Popes, now used as a barrack, and the cathedral, then continued our homeward journey arriving in Paris on Saturday night and once more taking up our abode at the Grande Hotel. I was so thankful to have a day's rest from travelling, as all our amusements of sightseeing, etc, had rather finished me up.

The first person I saw in Church on Sunday was Fred Wilkinson, so we joined him after service and he walked home with us. Left on Monday morning 11th February for Amiens, staying a night there to inspect the cathedral, which was beautiful. Crossed the Channel next day and in a few hours were in the arms of the Bolton Gardenites, Mother and Eliza having consumed our moon of honey, which we voted to have been a most sweet one.

Part Seven
Married Life

For a long time has this journal been closed, even until Sept 25 1869 when I again open it to record the birth of our little girl, to be christened some day soon, we hope, by the name of Una Josephine Mary. She was born at 8.35 on Sunday morning, September 5th, and was declared to be as large as many a one of two months old, and to be a beauty by the nurse's account, but to which proposition I could not assent, as I only saw a little red thing with a huge nose and inflamed-looking eyes and a bald head with just a shade of fluff upon it. But ugly though she might be, she is a treasure, and one much longed for, a sort of cornerstone to an arch of many blessings and mercies which have come to us since our marriage.

At the end of 67, I thought no year could be a happier one, but much happiness has been granted us since then. September 21st, 1868, was a day of great mercy, and a prayer was granted which had long been asked. There were also many clouds towards the end of that year, only sent as trials to faith and then mercifully removed. Herbert's work at the bar had been but very little, and there were only very poor accounts of coming business for 69, making us very anxious, but our prayers were again answered and more than double the business of last year was given to Herbert this spring. Then Fan was very ill, but she has been spared to us and though not very strong yet is pretty well again.

I have also some sorrows to record. First, dear old Kit's death on the 7th of February, the first break in our 13, but we know that she is only taken Home, and we cannot wish her home again. Then little Walter Moor's death of scarletina and diphtheria combined only a few days after Kit was taken.

Milly Morris has also been called away on the 17th

of August, but in each case one could trace the loving
Hand that sent the sorrow and His love and mercy
have been wonderful up to the present time.

My married life has been so happy, and I can never be thankful enough for my precious husband, and now for my little Una who has just come in from her first walk in the garden. She gave her first smile to her Papa on the day she was a month old. She was Christened on October 6th at St Mary's, the Boltons, by Mr Du Boulay, Walter, Daffie and Eliza being sponsors, but as Daffie could not be present, Mama was proxy for her.

On the 4th day of her existence, I told Mrs Husted she would have a strong will, and though much laughed at at the time for such an early prophesy, it has turned out quite true. After she was Christened she had a dreadful illness, beginning by thrush, then coming out in erysipelas in the head which spread all over her face, and she would lie for hours almost torpid on the nurse's knee, only moaning when moved. Dr Christian and Dr West saw her and said she must have a wet nurse, so Flory found for us Elizabeth MacKay, under whose nursing she recovered wonderfully, but for many days we thought there was no hope, and O the agony of that thought.

Una first stood alone at Kilnwick early in August 1870, when she pulled herself up by the petticoats of the nursery armchair. From Kilnwick we took her on with us to Scotland, and at Southwick she used to creep about with the Mark Stewarts' little boy, who afterwards died of scarlet fever. One day she seized his toy and crept away with it as hard as she could. He crept after her and bumped her head with a basket by way of punishment, on which she crept off to Silky and looked up pitifully, rubbing her head as if to get sympathy.

She said Ma-ma at 10 months and Pa pa and Ta Ta followed soon afterwards. She soon learnt many sweet little ways: sitting on a stool, she would hug her doll and rock it backwards and forwards to put it to sleep. She was devoted to music and would listen to it for any time, but there was generally a cry before she could be got to leave the piano. When she was old enough to walk to it, she would go and softly strike one note, then peep round at me to see what I thought of it, and if I smiled she would go on to strike 2 or 3 more, but I never let her strum. She was always a merry little thing, and dearly loved a game of play. She used to pretend to make her food as Silky made it, pretending to stir it in a box with a Noah out of an Ark for a spoon.

On the 23rd of February 1871, at 3 pm, little Maude Irene was born. She had a thick crop of dark hair, and when measured a few days after was 22 inches long. Una said "Sister" quite distinctly when told to do so in the afternoon, and seemed much amused at the new arrival, but evidently thought she was a doll. Una was put on my bed, and the baby was laid on her lap, which delighted her immensely.

Maude was Christened on the 4th of May at St Mary's, and behaved perfectly until her bonnet was replaced for going away. Her Godmothers were Lily and Maudie, and Francis Tottenham was proxy for Reggie who was on his way from India. Little Maude first smiled at a fortnight and 2 days old, and seems intending to be as merry as Una.

Una's first tooth came at 4 months, Maudie's at 4 1/2 months. Una tries to be a little mother to Maude, and tries to amuse her by dancing about or saying Quack Quack. Sometimes she strokes her so gently and says "Babee". She was so charmed the other night when she was in bed by Herbert putting Maude into her bed. She put her arms round her and cuddled her so tenderly. She delights also in pretending to carry her into my room, Herbert holding baby all the time, and Maude seems quite to enter into the joke. When Baby was put into her bed, Una offered her the blanket in which she likes to bury her own nose.

I have written this on July 23rd 71, Una being 1 year 10

1/2 months. She understands perfectly all that is said to her and is very obedient, though she has wilful and passionate fits sometimes. She can say many words, and a few little sentences, knows many of the people in my photo book and delights in finding out Papa among the pictures. She chatters immensely in her own way, and takes a book and pretends to read, talking gibberish all the time in a sensible tone. She seems inclined to be methodical and tidy, always puts away her toys and what she does one day, she likes to do another.

And here the journal suddenly stops. Whether this was the end of Octavia's writing activities, I do not know. She died 55 years later, in 1926, at the age of 82, having been a widow for more than three decades.

Printed in Great Britain
by Amazon